Knolly
from
Don

Lyme
2 July 1970

LEWIS
AND
CLARK

WILLIAM CLARK   MERIWETHER LEWIS

LEWIS AND CLARK

The Great Adventure

Illustrated

by Donald Barr Chidsey

CROWN PUBLISHERS, INC., NEW YORK

By the Same Author

HISTORY

Goodbye to Gunpowder
The Birth of the Constitution
July 4, 1776
Valley Forge
The Battle of New Orleans
Victory at Yorktown
The Great Separation
The Tide Turns
The Siege of Boston
The War in the North
The Great Conspiracy
The War with Mexico
The California Gold Rush
The French and Indian War
The War in the South

BIOGRAPHY

Elizabeth I
A Great Life in Brief

John the Great
The Times and Life of John L. Sullivan

The Gentleman from New York
A Biography of Roscoe Conkling

Sir Humphrey Gilbert
Elizabeth's Racketeer

Sir Walter Raleigh
That Damned Upstart

Marlborough
The Portrait of a Conqueror

Bonnie Prince Charlie
A Biography of the Young Pretender

Contents

LEWIS
AND
CLARK

1

Mammoths in the Transriverine Wilderness?

Bones fascinated Thomas Jefferson. The gift most welcome at the White House while the third President was ensconced there was a bag of bones, preferably prehistoric, which he could examine and about which he could spin theories. Nothing pleased him so much as fossils. He had never been west, never more than a few miles in that direction from his beloved Monticello, in Albemarle County, Virginia, but he speculated endlessly upon what lay beyond the mountains, or, better, beyond the Mississippi River. Almost *anything* might be there. He had the bones to prove it.

André Michaux was a botanist and a Frenchman, and in both capacities he was of exceptional interest to Thomas Jefferson, who had been secretary of state at the time Michaux proposed to head an expedition into that vast unknown called Louisiana. Jefferson gave him every conceivable encouragement, and even wrote out a list of suggestions, among them that Michaux might keep an eye open for mammoths, which could be thought still to roam the Louisiana country, for hadn't bits of their bones been found in Kentucky? Jefferson had added that it was by no means certain that that helpful beast the Peruvian llama had not strayed as far north as Louisiana, and Michaux was advised to watch out for it as well.

Nothing came of the proposed Michaux expedition into the mystery land, for the man turned out to be less interested in the flora and fauna of the transriverine wilderness than he was in promoting an independence movement in Tennessee, Kentucky, Ohio, and other regions between the mountains and the Mississippi, preferring to pry them loose from the United States rather than see them fall to Great Britain by conquest from the north. And when his patron, Citizen Genêt, the French ambassador at Washington, came into disgrace with the new and excessively energetic French Republic, the whole business blew up in Michaux's face. Thomas Jefferson, however, did not lose interest.

It had not been the first such failure. A young Connecticut Yankee named Ledyard had approached Jefferson in Paris some years earlier, when Jefferson was the American ambassador to France, with the request for aid to penetrate the land west of the Mississippi, *terra incognita*. It was a request Jefferson was never likely to brush aside, nor did he do so now.

John Ledyard was a notably persistent man. Whether he had reasons of his own for getting to the mysterious midregion between the Mississippi and the Pacific, or whether he was moved by sheer high spirits, does not matter; he stuck to the task. He traveled all the way to St. Petersburg, virtually a forbidden city then, as remote as Lhasa and twice as cold. Catherine the Great happened to be away from her capital, but Ledyard, a glib one, managed to talk two of her ministers into giving him passports to visit eastern Siberia, where he hoped to board some Russian fur-trade ship to the west coast of North America. He actually reached Siberia, but before he could arrange for further transporta-

PRESIDENT THOMAS JEFFERSON

tion the Empress Catherine got back to St. Petersburg, learned what had happened in her absence, and sent a couple of officers to seize the presumptive young American and bring him back.

It is not likely that Catherine had anything personal against John Ledyard, but she did not fancy the idea of foreign agents getting a look at the inside workings of Russia. At any rate, Ledyard was kicked out, and he went to Paris and waited upon the American ambassador there. His plan now was to attack the unknown land from the east, making a trip from the Father of Waters to the Pacific. Would Mr. Jefferson help him? Mr. Jefferson assuredly would.

However, before either of them could act, John Ledyard died—of natural causes—and that slowed the urge to explore. There were not many men alive who would even permit themselves to dream about Louisiana, much less go there.

Louisiana was a great geographic sprawl. Much of its southernmost boundary was either the Gulf of Mexico or the province of Texas, and all its easternmost boundary was the Mississippi River, but nobody knew how far north it extended, or how far west. Nobody knew; but many cared.

Great Britain had not yet begun to stammer, apologetically, that she had conquered half the world in a fit of absent-mindedness. She was still *outspokenly* greedy, and, in particular, greedy for land. She had recently taken all Canada from France, as spoils of war, and nobody doubted that Canada extended west as far as the Pacific. The question was, how far *south* did it extend? English and Scottish fur traders, an enterprising lot, baffled by the long and terrible winters that shut off their traffic for so much of the year, were eyeing with outright avarice land that might have been a part of Louisiana, land to the south of the St. Lawrence–Great Lakes line. They were doing more: they were penetrating that land, in small groups, to be sure, and making friends with some of the Indians, obviously with future operations in mind.

British skippers, too, men like Puget and Vancouver, were poking into dents along the Pacific coastline, following up the work of such maritime giants as Drake and Cook. One of these skippers had sent a lieutenant far up the great river that was believed to be the veritable River of the West, though an American, Captain Robert Gray of Boston, asserted that he had discovered this stream, which he named after his own vessel, the *Columbia.*

The Russians, too, not averse to a little land-grabbing of their own, were poking *down* the Pacific coast of North America in much the same manner that the British were poking *up,* and they had already established a fur-trading station on Nootka Sound.

The Spaniards somewhat plaintively claimed just about everything west of the Mississippi as a part of New Spain. Louisiana proper, whatever that was—the line between it and New Spain, the western border of Louisiana, was especially fuzzy—had been ceded to Spain at the end of the Seven Years' War, chiefly in order to keep it from annexation by an already gorged Great Britain. Spain was weak, on land and sea alike, and could be expected to keep Louisiana weak, not, as France would have done, strong.

The Spaniards did little or nothing about cutting in on the fur trade, but they did set up a few military posts, specifically St. Louis on the Mississippi at the mouth of the Missouri, and New Orleans. By controlling New Orleans, Spain which also controlled East Florida and West Florida, could, any time it wished, choke off the new American states of Kentucky, Ohio, and Tennessee—the fifteenth, sixteenth, and seventeenth members of the Union.

What could these new westerners do, what could the

others in less-well-organized colonies do—and more were pouring through the mountain gaps all the time to join them —if they did not have the use of the Mississippi? They were poor; they could not support one another. That they should send their products back through the same passes through which they themselves had just come, back to the states of the eastern seacoast, was unthinkable. Such a market, not in miles but in difficulties, was farther from them than the Gulf of Mexico; and if Spain were to shut the *entrepôt* of New Orleans to them, as Spain more than once had threatened to do, they would be ruined. They knew this, and they were muttering, a discontent that Spanish spies were quick to encourage.

If the hardy residents of Tennessee, Ohio, and Kentucky, together with those of adjacent American territories, were to break away from the United States, that would suit New Spain's book perfectly. A rickety, squabbling, split pair of republics on her eastern flank would be preferable to the growing might of the original group. And these western states *were* murmuring, *were* talking openly of secession, at just about the time that Thomas Jefferson moved into the White House. He knew this. It was very much in his mind.

The situation was made even more complicated by the emergence into the maelstrom that was European politics of a short, swart, and exceedingly tough Corsican soldier by the name of Napoleon Bonaparte, who had taken over France with the title of First Consul. This upstart was unpredictable. Scruples never even brushed him, and such was his duplicity that it caused even hardened diplomats to blanch. Moreover, he was now the master of Louisiana.

Bonaparte did not like peace; it made him uneasy. And he was deep in plans to renew hostilities against perfidious Albion, the place he castigated as "a nation of shopkeepers." He dreamed of a French empire that would include not only a large chunk of the West Indies but also Louisiana, with control of the mouth of the Mississippi. Only in this way, he believed, could France gain mastery of the sea. Left to herself, Napoleon reasoned, England would wrest Louisiana from Spain and use it as a bulwark against American expansion. Ergo: he himself should take Louisiana, which would be safe only in his hands. He did it. He arranged for the retrocession by means of simple threats. France had an enormous army.

The treaty of San Ildefonso was signed by France and Spain on October 1, 1800. It was supposed to be secret, but it was not a very well kept secret. Spanish troops still paraded at New Orleans and at St. Louis, and the Spanish flag flew over these towns, but nobody was fooled. Bonaparte could have the property any time he pressed for delivery of the deed.

It was therefore to Paris rather than to Madrid—where indeed the United States maintained no permanent ambassador—that President Jefferson sent when he sought to open negotiations for the purchase of New Orleans. To be sure, Bonaparte had made a solemn pledge to Spain at the time of the retrocession that he would not permit a single foot of this vast territory to fall into the hands of any other nation, but what of it? Bonaparte took seriously what Dean Swift had meant only in fun when he observed that promises and pie-crust were made to be broken.

It was true, too, that Jefferson was a "strict constructionist," which meant that he did not believe the federal government or any member of it could do anything that it or he was not specifically authorized to do in the constitution adopted in Philadelphia, Monday, September 17, 1787; and certainly this did not include the purchase of land from European powers. But he was of a pragmatic turn of mind, and the situation in the west was grave; so he sent his orders.

ROBERT R. LIVINGSTON

The American ambassador at Paris was Robert Livingston, of the New York Livingstons, a holdover Federalist. Party feeling was strong, and it was doubtful that the Republican-controlled Senate would ratify any treaty negotiated by a Federalist. This no doubt was the principal reason that, early in 1803, President Jefferson sent his fellow Virginian, young James Monroe, to Paris to assist Livingston—and to snatch all the glory. Even before Monroe got there the silken, iridescent Charles Maurice de Talleyrand-Périgord, French foreign minister, with the utmost casualness one morning asked if perhaps the United States might be interested in buying not merely New Orleans but all of Louisiana, a territory five times as big as France itself. Livingston, stunned for an instant, hastily accepted. By the time Monroe arrived, a few days later, these two were settling details. Monroe joined in. He had no more authority to do this than had Livingston, but they reasoned, sensibly, that it might take as long as half a year to write to Washington and get the Presidential permission to embrace an offer nobody could have dreamed would be made; and in that time the mercurial First Consul (for the offer certainly came from Bonaparte: Prince Talleyrand, whom the First Consul hated but needed, would never have dared to advance it on his own responsibility) might well have changed his mind.

2

The Biggest Real Estate Deal in History

Bonaparte's decision, though unexpected, was clear enough after the event. The Negro residents of the island of Hispaniola, which France shared with Spain (which means that France owned it), having been freed and then by order of Bonaparte enslaved again, had revolted. The result was holocaustal. Expensively trained French soldiers were lost by the thousands to Haitian knives and to disease. Never one to hesitate about ditching a lost cause,[1] Bonaparte gave up Hispaniola, and by doing so he gave up all immediate hope of holding the Louisiana territory he had not yet officially annexed. He could not hold Louisiana without Hispaniola, but if he couldn't have it he wished to make sure that Great Britain didn't get it. Britain might readily have wrested it from the weak Spain—for Spain soon would be forced into the war-to-come: this was a part of Bonaparte's plan—but Britain would never dare to embroil herself with the new American republic while still engaged in a death grapple with France. So much for Napoleon Bonaparte's

The Louisiana Purchase—Monroe and Livingston

COMPLETING NEGOTIATIONS WITH TALLEYRAND, APRIL 30, 1803

reasons—though it might be added that he could use the
cash, too.

'The haggling also involved American spoliation claims
left from the recent Franco-American undeclared sea war,
not to mention certain French counter-claims, and also the
difference in money values between the franc and the dollar;
but when all snarls had been straightened, and three separate
conventions had been signed, April 30 and May 2, 1803,
what the agreement amounted to was that the United States
would pay a little over $27,260,000 for Louisiana.

Calling the territory about one million square miles—
a very conservative estimate—this would make the price four
cents an acre.

It was the biggest real estate deal in history.

Three separate couriers took three separate copies of
the conventions by three separate ships, each of them reputed
to be fast, but it was July 14 of that year before President
Jefferson in Washington was apprised of the fact that—if he
could get the Senate to agree—his country was about to be
doubled in size. He got the Senate to agree.

Meanwhile, and never dreaming that his representatives
would bring home such a big bundle, Jefferson had gone
ahead with his plans to invade what he could only think of
as foreign territory. Anything but a bold man—physically,
that is—he was about to embark upon a course that would
have given any general pause. Moreover, he was about to
do this with the United States Army, of which constitution-
ally he was commander-in-chief. No longer would he rely
upon civilians like Ledyard and Michaux.[2]

Geographers were saying that there must be a continent
in the far southern part of the globe—despite the failure of
even James Cook to find it—for the simple reason that in the
absence of such a land mass the earth would be lopsided
and would wobble wildly as it spun on its axis. In a like man-

ner it was perfectly apparent and always had been that there must be four cardinal rivers in North America, one flowing in each of the four directions. Assuredly the Mississippi was the River of the South, as the St. Lawrence was the River of the East. The stream Alexander Mackenzie had lately discovered, and that was named after him, could easily be considered the River of the North, since he had followed it clear to the Arctic Ocean. Where, then, was the River of the West? There had to be one. This was patent even to a mind as clear as that of Thomas Jefferson. Everybody accepted it.

Could it be the Columbia? This seemed likely. Little was known about the mouth of the Columbia, which so recently had been discovered, and nothing whatever was known about the rest of it; but it was a big river and it flowed in a westerly direction.

The dream of a northwestern water passage from the Atlantic to the Pacific had haunted the minds of men for more than three hundred years. Few still believed that a *continuous* passage would ever be found, but it was altogether possible, some said, that the portage between the upper waters of the Missouri and the upper waters of the River of the West would be a short one. It was known—Indians had attested to it—that there were mountains to the west; but it was not believed that these constituted a formidable block. The principal duty of Mr. Jefferson's expedition would be to determine this.

He was at pains to impress upon everybody involved that the United States Army was to be used only because it was there, it was convenient, and that this was to be by no means a military maneuver, much less an act of war. He called its purpose "literary," by which he meant "scientific," "fact-finding." He explained this, very carefully, to the British, French, and Spanish ministers stationed in Washington, before he approached Congress with the proposition. Nevertheless, his message to Congress, January 18, 1803, was marked "secret." He wanted no fanfare.[3]

He told Congress that he thought "an intelligent officer with ten or twelve chosen men, fit for the enterprize and willing to undertake it," would be enough. Then, no doubt holding his breath, appalled by his own temerity, he asked for a special appropriation of $2,500 to cover everything.

The "confidential" message made much of the need for domesticating the Indians, who were getting restless as their land was being taken from them in increasingly massive chunks, and it asserted that the expedition would do much toward this end. "The extensive forests necessary in the hunting life, will then become useless, & they will see advantage in exchanging them for the means of improving their farms, & of increasing their domestic comforts," the President wrote. Well, maybe. Thomas Jefferson was a humane man, and a farlooking one, and nobody doubted that he had the Indians in mind. But nobody doubted, either, that his first thought was the chance of rerouting the lucrative fur trade through the United States; and it could be that certain foreign powers would not approve of this.

If there was a discussion on the floor, if the request met resistance, Congress managed to keep this quiet. The President, after all, had a firm grip on both houses, and the natural opposition, the Federal party, already jejune, was tottering toward extinction. Jefferson got his grant.

There was never any mystery about who would lead this expensive jaunt. The President had talked it over time after time with Meriwether Lewis, a neighbor from Virginia, who held the rank of captain in the army, from which he had been given a leave of absence to act as Mr. Jefferson's secretary.

Lewis was twenty-nine years old, and by no means a

typical army man. He was introverted, given to moods of melancholia. *Physically* as tough as they come, he kept to himself much of the time. He was not good company, though he was efficient and thorough in everything he did.

After his appointment, it was Lewis himself who immediately asked the President to appoint his friend William Clark to become a sort of adjutant or coleader, and to get the army to give Clark a captaincy for this occasion. They were good friends. Clark, a young brother of George Rogers Clark, the West-country hero, was a few years older than Lewis—he was thirty-three—and Lewis actually had served under him for a few months. Since that time Clark had resigned his lieutenancy, nor was he on the reserve list. Mr. Jefferson assured his young friend that this could easily be done, and he so notified the War Department. The War Department, however, for reasons of its own, decided that it could offer Clark not a captaincy, as requested by the President, but only a second lieutenancy, as an artillerist unattached; and this it did, and Clark accepted.

Rank never mattered between these two men. Clark was looked upon as a captain, Lewis's equal in everything. He was addressed as captain and so signed himself, though without adding a regimental designation, as Lewis invariably did.

Clark was by almost four years the senior, but he seems never to have been irked by his position as second-in-command, a position of which his partner never reminded him.

Clark's people originally had been Scottish, Lewis's Welsh. Each was the son of a moderately wealthy frontier planter, and each had been rather scantily educated, though they were as "lettered" as others of their place and generation, technically gentlemen, if not *polished* gentlemen. Their backgrounds, then, were similar. Their dispositions decidedly were not.

William Clark

Meriwether Lewis

Clark had light blue eyes and bright red hair and a quick grin. *He* was an extrovert, the opposite of the other. He was also a qualified map maker.

Clark was the youngest of six brothers, and all five of the others had served as officers in the Revolution, something that William was too young to get into. The youngest son had, it is true, seen service against the Indians on the frontier, under the redoubtable "Mad Anthony" Wayne. Lewis had seen no action at all. Lewis's home life must have been much different from that of the outgoing, gregarious Clark. An only son, he was adored by his one sister, Jane, and by his widowed mother, Mary. He liked to read poetry, alone. He liked to take long walks in the woods.

Both families had settled in the western part of Virginia, but the Clarks, even before William was born, had moved to Kentucky.

William Clark had been brought up in the shadow of the fame of his older brothers, and especially that of the oldest of them, George Rogers Clark, *the* frontier hero of the Revolution; but this did not seem to depress or to awe him, for he was invariably pleasant, easy to meet. Meriwether Lewis, on the other hand, preferred his own company.

Neither could be called a handsome man, but both were tall, which counted with the Indians. Lewis was slightly bowlegged.

Each, but particularly Clark, had had experience with river craft. Each was a crack shot.

Most important of all was the fact that, though they were of such widely differing personalities, they got along perfectly. Without any sentimental overtones, without ever sounding a Damon-and-Pythias note, this was one of the great friendships of history. There was never to be a sign of jealousy, not even a touch of querulousness, or testiness, over the long years that they were in close contact. They knew each other, understood each other, trusted each other, which proved to be a fine thing for the country.

The first step, once the permission of Congress had been gained, was to issue a long set of instructions to Meriwether Lewis. These authorized him to raise "arms for your attendants, say for from 10 to 12 men, boats, tents, & other travelling apparatus, with ammunition, medicine, surgical instruments & provisions you will have prepared with such aids as the Secretary of War can yield in his department." He was to use his own judgment in treating with the Indians. He was to make reports on the various rivers he passed and on the flora and fauna of the countryside that bordered them, though no mention was made of the mammoth, nor yet of the Peruvian llama. "Should you reach the Pacific ocean," the instructions continued, he was to tell off two of his men, give them the reports of the expedition, and instruct them to seek passage on some fur-trading vessel for a return by sea, around the Cape of Good Hope, to the United States; but if he thought it might be too dangerous to return by the way he had come he was authorized to take the *entire expedition* back by sea, provided vessels were available, and for this purpose he was to be equipped with letters of credit to various United States consuls in far parts of the world.

These instructions [4] were actually issued June 20, 1803, but Lewis certainly had been familiar with them before this, for he had helped to frame them. They made no mention of William Clark.

As soon as the project had become certain, Lewis, whose duties as secretary to so prodigious a worker as President Jefferson must have been light, betook himself to the country's center of learning and culture, the city sometimes called the Athens of the West, and in Philadelphia he studied, somewhat hastily, celestial navigation, mineralogy, and related subjects, and took a course in elementary surgery and medicine under the renowned Dr. Benjamin Rush.

He was already on his way west—he had left Washington July 5—when there came to the capital the momentous news that the United States had purchased not only the city of New Orleans but also the entire territory of Louisiana.

Now the need for secrecy was gone, for the expedition had suddenly become "legitimate." At least, the first part of it had become so. Nobody knew how Spain and Great Britain, not to mention Russia, might view the establishment of an American military base on the Pacific coast, for it was generally understood, at least, that the Louisiana territory did not extend this far. And of course nobody knew how the Indians would act.

3

Glass Beads for the Natives

WHAT TO PACK, always a problem for the inexperienced traveler and especially if he plans to embark for lands unknown, could never have been a question so acute as it was with Meriwether Lewis in the spring and summer of 1803. A perfectionist by nature, he was desperately anxious to have this expedition prove a success. After all, in order to make it he had given up a $600-a-year job, the presidential secretaryship.

Pittsburgh was to be his jumping-off place, but he gathered his supplies from many sources—New York, Washington, the government arsenal at Harpers Ferry, most of all from the quartermaster general's depot at Philadelphia.

Some of these were what might have been expected—for instance, he took twenty-one bales of Indian gifts such as beads, looking glasses, curtain rings, coins. Others were ideas of his own. He stocked heavily with what he listed as "portable soup," and which was evidently powdered soup, something new. The men were not to like this, and were to refuse it except on such occasions—and there were to be many of them—when they teetered on the very verge of starvation; but at the time, Captain Lewis thought it an excellent idea. And there was the *Experiment*.

Experiment was an iron boat of his own devising.[5] It was really only the frame of a boat, made to his specifications at Harpers Ferry, Virginia, and the plan was that when it was needed it could be covered with fresh bark, preferably birch bark. It was thirty-six feet long, four and one-half feet in beam, and twenty-six inches deep, and it would draw very little, he reckoned. It came apart for easy carrying. Broken down, it weighed only a few hundred pounds, but Lewis calculated that it was capable of carrying an eight thousand-pound load when assembled and put into the water. He was very proud of it.

The keelboat in which he planned to make the major part of his trip, and which he had ordered in advance from a Pittsburgh builder, was a more conventional vessel; but it too had its unusual points, and Captain Lewis was fussy about them. It had ten-foot decks fore and aft, with a forecastle and an after cabin. Amidships, the gunwales were backed by stout wooden lockers that could be raised to make them higher in the event of an Indian attack from either shore. There was also a huge tarpaulin that could be fastened into place in a matter of minutes and would protect the waist against the highest waters the Missouri might throw at it. The vessel itself could be poled or rowed, though poling was easiest if the river was not too deep. There was also a square sail mounted on a thick stumpy mast for the stretches.

All this should have been ready when Captain Lewis rode into Pittsburgh early on the afternoon of July 15. It was not. It had barely been begun. The contractor, it developed, was overfond of his bottle, and when he was not drunk he was likely to be sleeping one off. Lewis raged. In a fury, he wrote to the President. He priced vessels in other yards, vainly. And he kept after the guilty builder. Why, they hadn't even started to make the poles and oars yet, a job that alone would take them twelve days!

Lewis's anxiety was more than just the excitement of a young man on the brink of his first command. Being behind schedule, at this stage, might conceivably be fatal to the whole enterprise. The Ohio, a tricky stream in its upper reaches, was falling every day. Soon it would be impassable. Already the great masses of brush and floating logs that the river men called "wooden islands" were increasing. Already the "riffles," shoal spots, were wider and more numerous. If he did not get going soon he might have to wait until spring.

He had been warned against the riffles of late summer, and he had taken some precautions. He chartered two wagons, with their drivers, to take some of the heaviest of the cargo by land as far as Wheeling, Virginia.[6] Below Wheeling, an enterprising port of more than a hundred houses, the river was more readily navigated.

He enlisted eleven boatmen, including a pilot, in Pittsburgh. He also had with him, as a personal bodyguard, six soldiers under a corporal.

His second choice for adjutant, after Clark, from whom he had not yet heard, was one Lieutenant Israel Hook, United States Army, another young man, stationed presently at a western fort. Lewis had asked him to stand by, to meet the expedition at the mouth of the Ohio, and to join it in the event that Clark decided to say no. Clark, however, a Virginian originally but now living in Louisville, Kentucky, said nothing of the sort. He avowed—and his letter reached Lewis in Pittsburgh—that he would be delighted to serve in the Corps of Discovery, as the expedition was carefully called. He made no reservations, sought no promises. There was no man in the world, he wrote rhapsodically, with whom he would sooner serve on such a mission.

Lewis wrote to Clark to join him at Louisville, and told

him that meanwhile he, Clark, might enlist some men—
Lewis himself already had enlisted three—for the Corps of
Discovery. Such enlistments, he stipulated in one of the rare
examples of his assertion of top leadership, must be subject
to his veto when he met the volunteers in person. Clark
should not solicit any "soft white hands." He was cautioned
against signing up any son of the rich who might be looking only for a thrill. They wanted none of those.

It was the last day of August before the party got under
way, a scant few hours after the finishing touches had
been put to the keelboat.

They were in trouble promptly. The riffles were even
worse than they had feared, and again and again all hands
had to be ordered overside to push and haul the big craft over
the shallow spots. It was backbreaking work.

It just so happened that near each of these bad spots
there lived a man who owned a pair of oxen or at least a
team of horses. These men were willing to help, for a price.
And the price was high. Lewis was called upon to give as
much as two dollars for a pair of animals and the services
of a driver on a job that might not take more than two or
three hours. He stormed; but he paid.

An unexpected cause of delays was the fogs, the heaviest
anybody ever had known in those parts. The weather on
the whole was fair, but there was fog almost every night,
and it was so thick that they could not navigate, nor could
they resume their journey the next morning until the sun
had burned it away, which sometimes was as late as eight
o'clock.

Two of the hands got so drunk in Marietta that they
had to be carried back aboard. Lewis did not fire them; but
he did fire two others at this same place, and he took on a
stout lad who was working his way west.

Lewis was not stingy with his Monongahela, but he

never did leave an open barrel on the deck with a tin dipper for anybody who wanted to help himself at any time, as most keelboat operators did. He would treat the men to a good stiff swallow after any arduous task or in chilly or rainy weather, but he did not subscribe to the belief, common then, that whiskey was necessary to keep up a laborer's strength.

At Cincinnati he lay over for five days, to give the men a rest. They had now come some five hundred miles, and the worst part of the river was behind them. Lewis himself used a part of this time to visit the nearby paleontological remains at Big Bone Lick, where he took many notes; afterward, he wrote a long letter about it to President Jefferson.[7]

They picked up Clark at Louisville on October 26, and it was a joyous occasion.

They were using the sail a great deal now, and were making good time. But Lewis took ill with a fever. He was not sure what the trouble was, but he rested and dosed himself with Dr. Rush's pills, in which he had great faith. Clark on this occasion—as indeed upon every occasion—was a mountain of strength.

They paused for a few days in November at Fort Massac, near the mouth of the river,[8] and there they hired Georges Drouillard, or Drewer, a famous hunter, son of a French Canadian and a Shawnee woman. Drewer was a valuable man. He was at home wherever the going was hardest, and he could be useful also as an interpreter. They paid him thirty dollars in advance, Lewis borrowing the money from the commanding officer at Fort Massac.

At the junction of the Ohio and the Mississippi they took soundings and pitched camp. The thing that most amazed them about this place was the size of the catfish the men so easily caught. One of them tipped the scales at 126 pounds. They were told—they did not say that they had *seen* this—that catfish there sometimes ran as heavy as 200 pounds. (Throughout this journey each of the captains was careful to report as fact, whether in his formal journal or less formal letters, only what he himself had *seen*. They were not gullible men, and they were properly careful about their material.)

Don Carlos Duhault Delassus, commander of the military post at St. Louis and governor of Upper Louisiana, knew about the stupendous sale. He knew that his official days were numbered. With the skimpy force at his command he could not hope to hold off the Americans if they came pouring into their new possessions, as he feared they would do. But he knew too—and he was a stubborn man—that he had not yet been officially informed of the Louisiana Purchase, and so it remained his duty to protect the place he held. When Captain Meriwether Lewis, United States Army, burst in upon him from some point downriver he firmly shook his head.

Lewis did not look belligerent. He wore his uniform, of course, and there was a dress sword strapped at his waist, but he was accompanied only by two interpreters, both civilians. He did not seem dismayed when Governor Delassus told him that in the circumstances he could not possibly grant him permission to go boating on the Missouri. True, the United States now owned all this territory *on paper*, but the United States did not own it *in fact*—not yet, anyway. Don Carlos could take orders only from the governor-general in New Orleans, who took *his* orders only from Charles IV himself. And that was that.

Lewis bowed, assenting. But immediately after that he began to pour questions over the governor like syrup, through the two civilians who attended him. The things the man didn't ask! He seemed *starved* for information! Cagey, Governor Delassus answered only a small portion of the ques-

tions, though he must have known that the deluge would
not cease. They were both polite, perfect gentlemen.

Lewis of course knew that it was too late—it was already
December—to start up the Missouri River. He would do
that first thing in the spring, by which time the Louisiana
territory would surely be United States property.

(The formal ceremony, actually, was to take place in St.
Louis on March 9, 1804, with Captain Lewis as one of those
representing the United States.)

Meanwhile, William Clark had explored the east bank
of the Mississippi and picked out a good place for a winter
encampment. It was on the Rivière Dubois, which they
already had Englished into Wood River, a stream that emptied into the Mississippi exactly opposite the mouth of the
Missouri.[9] It was about eighteen miles from St. Louis, and
was particularly desirable because of the large number of
wild animals, especially turkeys and 'possums, in the neighborhood. There they settled.

Their numbers varied throughout that winter, but they
were probably never more than forty. Not all these were
members of the Corps of Discovery; some were regular
soldiers assigned to protect the others as far as their next
winter quarters and to return with samples and letters;
others were civilians—boatmen, interpreters, and the like.

Delassus liked Captain Lewis and trusted him, but the
Spaniards to the south—in New Orleans, in Sonora, Chi-
huahua, Santa Fe—were not so sure. The wildest sorts of
stories were circulated among them about that camp on
Wood River. Clark and Lewis were "soldiers' soldiers," and
insisted upon the most stringent discipline among the rather
raffish collection of enlistees from this post and from that.
The camp was loud all day with challenges, countersigns,
and the clack of presented arms. The Spaniards to the south,
hearing exaggerated tales about these doings, took alarm.

They did not know, any more than did anybody else, where the Missouri started or how far it stretched and in what direction; but was it not possible that "Capitán Merry Whether" might venture up some long southern tributary of the Missouri, some stream as yet unknown, and in this manner make his way uninvited into the Santa Fe country?

In a questionnaire Lewis had caused to be made up in French as well as in English and to be handed to every fur dealer he could find who had ever ascended any part of the Missouri, he had been specific about minerals: "What are your mines and minerals? Have you lead, iron, copper, pewter, gypsum, salts, salines, or other mineral waters, nitre, stone-coal, marble, limestone, or any other mineral substance?" He never mentioned gold and silver, and probably never thought of them. The Spaniards, on the other hand, thought of little else.

The governor of Santa Fe decided to take steps. He sent out a force of more than sixty men, militia and regulars, under Don Pedro Vial, who had orders to find the headwaters of the Arkansas River and follow this river down to the Missouri, thus effectively cutting off "Capitán Merry Whether" and his dastardly intruders. The Spanish force did reach the Arkansas, but there it was attacked by a much larger force of Indians—not Pawnees, with whom the Spaniards had a treaty—they did not seem to know *what* Indians these were—who were driven off only after they had cut the camp to pieces and stolen a large part of the supplies. The Spanish force returned to Santa Fe. There had never been a confrontation. Clark and Lewis did not even hear about this business until several years later.

The original plan had called for an officer and ten or twelve men, but this soon was found to be inadequate. The two captains knew that what they needed, at least for the first part of the expedition, to take them through the danger-

ous Sioux country, was a force of about forty. Fewer would
be unsafe. More would pose a supply problem.

The heart of the force was the so-called nine young
men from Kentucky. Two of these had been picked by Lewis,
the remaining seven by Clark at Louisville. The youngest
was eighteen, the oldest thirty-three. They were all sworn
into the regular army. In addition, there were fourteen army
privates, chosen largely for their skills. Three sergeants were
picked out of these by the captains. There was Clark's personal servant, a Negro. There were a corporal and six privates, destined to return with mail and samples after the
first winter in the field. And finally there were nine *engagés*,
all French—boatmen, interpreters, hunters.

There had been a few others in the camp at Wood River,
but these either had been sent back to their posts as un-
satisfactory or had changed their minds and slipped into the
forest. Desertion was easy in that wild country.

This, then, was the force as the captains wanted it and
had sought to make it. On the afternoon of May 14, 1804,
it pushed across the Mississippi and straight into the maw of
the huge brown rolling Missouri.

The great adventure had begun.

It was a Monday, and it was raining.

CHAPTER

4

Boldly Into the Unknown

THE RIVER WAS AN ENEMY. It was implacable. It
squirmed incessantly, never still, always sullen, always alert
for a chance to strike. There were races. There were eddies.
There were sudden, inexplicable surface boils. Again and
again the river turned back upon itself, so that it seemed
all curves, and the curves were the most dangerous parts of
this dangerous, evil-purposed stream. The Missouri was always slashing at the curves, straightening itself, and this
process, which could happen without warning, often sent
tons of mud swirling downstream in a matter of minutes—
enough to swamp a small boat, to badly rock a raft.

The river had not yet been dubbed the Big Muddy,
the name by which later generations were to know it, but it
is likely that the Lewis-Clark men called it many a harsher
thing.

It was strong, and seemed determined to resist all pen-
etration. If they made thirty miles, whether by sail, sweeps,
or poles, or a combination of any two or all three of these,
that was a memorable day. Sometimes they made only five
or six.

WILLIAM CLARK'S COMPASS, ON A WATCH CHAIN

Poling was possible only close to the shore, but that was the place of the greatest peril. Even where the bend was almost imperceptible the convex side was likely to be under-washed, eaten away beneath the surface, so that the whole bank would collapse with a crash, taking with it any cockle-shell that chanced to be near.

They never traveled at night. When they camped it was sometimes on river islands, but they had to keep careful watch, for the island itself might suddenly break up like an iceberg and go floating, in sections, downstream. When they camped along the banks they got far back from the edge.

Avoiding the neighborhood of the banks when the ex-

pedition was on the move was not always possible, because
of the enormous *embarras,* or mats of driftwood. Sometimes
these could be very large, seas of floating timber, extending
for miles upstream and down, and almost from one bank to
the other. At their best they were an impediment to be
fought through. At their worst they were clogged with
floating, whirling trees, only a small part of which showed
above the surface.

The river was provident. It gave of its life gladly, fur-
nishing all manner of fish almost as fast as the line was cast,
the hook dropped. There were pike, bass, trout, rockfish,
perch, flatback, silverfish, and a sort of salmon, besides
plenty of shrimp and mussels, and most of all there were the
catfish, which ran bigger than anybody in the party had
ever seen before. Yes, the river was provident. But—you
didn't dare turn your back on it.

The first town they came upon—the first and last except Indian villages—was the tiny trading post of La Charette. This was the very outer rim of civilization, and they
stopped there for a few hours to restow some of their cargo.
If they met the syndic, the magistrate, they made no mention of the fact in their diaries and letters. He might have
been out taking care of his traps and gunning for some more
game, for though he was seventy years old he was still active.
His name was Daniel Boone.

The *engagés* were illiterate, but the soldiers made up
the writingest crew conceivable. The two captains were
scribbling a good part of the time, recording everything—
the depth and the color of the water, its speed, the nature
of the banks, the animals, the plants, everything—and from
these field notes they would later, in camp, write up a more
considered journal. The expedition had two horses, and
often one of the captains—usually it was Lewis, a prodigious
walker—would go along a bank with these, just for the exer-

cise; and in that case the other captain, seated in the keel-boat, more often than not would be jotting down notes on a folding desk. Clark, in addition, did a lot of map-making. Sometimes he did this under trying conditions. A high wind blew away all his notes on one occasion, and on another the rocking of the boat caused a whole bottle of ink to spill over his papers; but he persisted.

In addition, the soldiers were urged to keep diaries, and seven of them did so. Most of their writing was done in camp, at dusk. Each of these efforts, even those of the two captains, was done separately, without conference or consultation. The captains would decide what names to give to new rivers or creeks, or new mountains, but the recording of those names was an every-man-for-himself operation. From the beginning they were piling up a formidable mass of reading matter. No matter what might happen to individual note-takers, *something* would surely survive.

The captains themselves were easily the most industrious of these diarists. They strove to be matter-of-fact, and much of what they put down was merely statistical, but from time to time they could not help slipping into poetry, rather homely poetry but effective. They seemed to have a passion, in particular, for streams. "A handsome little river . . . a bold, deep creek" are phrases that often occur. The captains were fascinated by "some cranes, the largest bird of that kind common to the Missouri and Mississippi, perfectly white except the large feathers on the first joint of the wing, which are black." [10] They were never so busy in matters of discipline and supply that they could not note things like the eggs of the large brown curlew, "a pale blue with small black specks, which she lays right on the ground having no nest," or record the interesting datum that the mating call of the male prairie hen sounded like *kuck, kuck, kuck, coo, coo, coo.*

Their spelling and punctuation, especially those of Clark, were execrable; but their meaning was clear.

On May 22, at Bonhomme Creek, which they Englished into Goodman's Creek, they came upon a hunting party of Kickapoos, men who would ordinarily be operating along the east bank of the Mississippi, where, however, as they reported, game was scarce at just that time. The explorers bought four fat deer from the Kickapoos, paying for them with two bottles of whiskey.

Early the following month their own hunters began to bring in food—black bear, venison, elk—and they reported seeing vast herds of buffalo at a great distance to the east and to the west.

They did not have the river to themselves. June 12 they encountered a raft loaded with furs and Frenchmen and headed southeast for St. Louis. There was much jabbering, which lasted most of the night, for the two captains wished to know everything that there was to know about the land ahead, up the river, and about the Indians that might be met.

Of the Mandans, who inhabited a cluster of villages high up along the Missouri, they heard only good things. The Mandans, the French averred, were good Indians. Of the Pawnees to the south and the Blackfeet to the north vague but terrible tales were told. More immediately troublesome, in fact just upstream a little way, were the Sioux, a thievish race of red men who seemed to regard the middle Missouri as their own private property and who tended to hold up the fur traders for "gifts" so insistently that the traders were thinking of quitting the big river entirely and making again for the Great Lakes–St. Lawrence route. Yes, watch out for the Sioux. They were unpleasant people.

An important result of this late-night confab was the signing up of one of the Frenchmen, Pierre Dorian, to turn around and go with the Lewis and Clark expedition up into

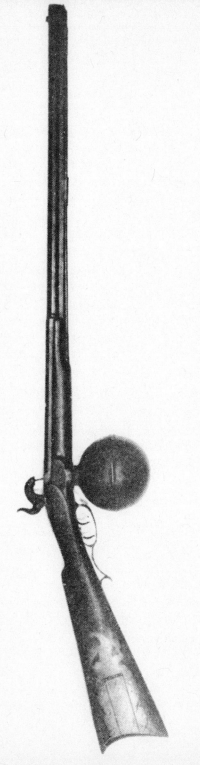

Courtesy of Montana Historical Society, Helena

AN AIR GUN USED BY THE LEWIS AND CLARK EXPEDITION

the Mandan country. Dorian knew the Mandans, spoke their language, had lived among them, and would be a valuable adjunct to the party.

June 26 they came to the mouth of one of the major tributaries of the Missouri, a river named the Kansas after the Indians who lived along its banks, though not near the mouth.[11] That was forty-four days from the day they had started.

John Collins and Hugh Hall, privates, were caught stealing whiskey, too much of which Collins already had drunk. Clark and Lewis wished to be, and at the camp on Wood River had striven to be, exceptionally strict in the matter of liquor. Still, they did not sit upon the court martial they themselves had summoned. This was made up entirely of enlisted men, who found Collins and Hall guilty, sentencing the first to one hundred lashes, the second to fifty. These sentences were carried out that very afternoon. (It should be noted that the army lash at that time, though a whippy weapon, was by no means the barbarous lead-studded cat-o'-nine-tails in use in the United States Navy. Few men could have taken a hundred lashes in the Navy without ending as gibbering idiots, or cripples, or corpses.)

July 4 they discovered two creeks, and named them, not unexpectedly, Independence and Fourth of July.

A few nights after that, five of the men were kept awake with splitting headaches, for which there was never to be an explanation. Some of the men had boils, and there was a certain amount of dysentery, but on the whole the health of the party had been good.

July 12 Private Alexander Willard was sentenced to a hundred lashes for sleeping on guard duty. Because this could have been punished by death both of the officers sat on the court-martial. The lashes were laid on over four different nights, twenty-five each time. The captains had no further trouble with Alexander Willard.

They had been out sixty-nine days when they came upon the mouth of yet another great river on their left, the west bank. This was the Platte, and they marveled at—as they measured—its shallowness, its width, its speed. This might have been called the *Greater* Muddy, for it was dark with sand.[12] The Missouri, they had determined, flowed at an average rate of six miles an hour, as compared with the Mississippi's four miles an hour, but the Platte flowed at *eight* miles an hour.

They had traveled about six hundred miles by that time.

CHAPTER

5

Grizzlies, Buffalo, Prairie Dogs

THE MISSOURI was even more crooked above the Platte, though the current was not so swift. The country was open now: there were more prairies, fewer woods.

Moses B. Reed, a private, and an *engagé* named La Liberté deserted, presumably together. La Liberté got away, and it was believed that he had found refuge among some Otos who were camped nearby; nobody in the party ever saw him again. Reed was pursued and captured at gunpoint. He was read out of the army and his pay was stopped. He was not allowed to do guard duty after that, but was given all the dirtiest jobs around the camping places. It was understood that he would be sent back to St. Louis as soon as this was practicable.

They made many side trips, though they never did get far from the Missouri itself. They visited the red-pipestone quarry on the Big Sioux, a place that was by common consent a neutral ground, no matter which tribes might be at war with which, it being such a convenient place for getting pipe material. All the Indians in those parts were heavy smokers, though their tobacco was poor stuff. A "carrot" of tobacco—a twist—was one of the most desirable presents the white men might give to the red.

On August 25, both of the captains and ten of the men hiked a considerable distance to the Mountain of the Little People. These creatures, averaging between eighteen inches and two feet in height, were ferocious fighters, according to the stories of sundry Mahas and Otos who had recently been encountered. The ordinary-sized Indians, Clark and Lewis were told, were frankly afraid of them. None, however, showed himself to the hikers; and the mountain itself, little more than a bump on the prairie, was not worth the trip.

Being extremely fond of beaver, both the pelt and the meat, and especially the tail, a delicacy, they often poked up creeks in search of dams. When, however, on July 31, some of the men brought a small live beaver back to camp and easily proceeded to tame it, there was a great deal of fear that Scammon might resent this.

Scammon—or Scannon, as he was also called—was Lewis's dog. He was a Newfoundland, a huge, black, shaggy one, devoted to his master. Everybody loved him; and once when he was bitten in the leg by a rattlesnake—he was not much good at sensing the presence of snakes, as some dogs are—the whole company worried about him for days, until he pulled through.

Scammon was no mutt. In the Indian villages he glittered like a true aristocrat, fascinating the natives. Lewis had paid twenty dollars for him. Early in the journey, still in the lower reaches of the Missouri, a Delaware had offered to give three beaver skins for him, an offer Lewis politely but firmly rejected.

There might have been times when even Meriwether Lewis wished that Scammon was a cat. He was no ratter.

It was not that he was afraid of them; but he was too slow. He was no mouser, either, and the mice, which infested the boats in even greater numbers, simply snickered at the well-meaning but clumsy Scammon. Mice and rats, but especially the mice, played hob with the cereal supplies, which had to be checked again and again. After the Lewis and Clark experience the word was to go out to all who planned a trip up the Missouri: Take a cat! No sane trader would start without one, and cats were rated high in St. Louis. But Clark and Lewis did not know this when they pushed forth. They had to learn the hard way.

Painted by Landseer, hymned by both Byron and Burns, the Newfoundland dog is thought of as admirable but not, on the whole, *useful.* Yet Scammon had his uses, aside from the charm of his company. He was an excellent watch dog. Just at first this did not mean much, for military methods were employed and there were sentries posted night and day at each encampment, sentries quick to challenge. However, when the party got far up the Missouri, in the land of the grizzlies, Scammon, who could smell a bear a long way off, much better than could any sentry, became decidedly helpful.

None of them had ever before seen a grizzly bear, or even heard of them, and Scammon at least took an instant dislike to the species, *Ursus horribilis,* and would go into a frenzy of barking at the first sniff of one. The grizzlies, for their part, though outweighing him at least four or five to one, showed a healthy respect for Scammon, and there were no incidents.

The diarists not always but often referred to these beasts as "white" bears. This was not because they believed them to be polar bears, *Ursus maritimus,* the nearest of which must have been a couple of thousand miles to the north, but to distinguish them from the commoner, smaller, and much less fierce black bears, with which they had previously been familiar. In fact the grizzly, then as now, was a yellowish gray or brown.

They were fierce animals, and, though heavy, very quick on their feet. The best thing to do when one of them chased you—and they would attack on sight—was to climb a tree. Adult grizzlies, being too heavy, could not climb. This happened to more than one member of the Lewis and Clark expedition. The grizzlies indeed were their bloodiest danger. Even the Indians never tackled a grizzly unless they numbered at least six in the party; and they never ate the meat unless they were starving.

Early in the journey Scammon had displayed an unexpected talent, which thereafter he never tired of exercising. He could retrieve. The breed was never meant for this, and nobody had *taught* Scammon, but the trick came to him suddenly, like a blinding light.

There was always bird life above—black cormorants, pelicans with their enormous beaks,[13] teal, pintails, greenheads, geese, mallards—and the two captains spent much of their time picking off birds, in part for sport, mostly for food. This called for a great deal of zigzagging, of stopping and starting, which wasted time. Scammon soon put a stop to that. Without having been ordered to, and with a mighty splash, one day he dove overboard, to come back with a fowl in his mouth. Then there was another, and another. Scammon was a powerful swimmer, and this was good exercise for him, besides being a good show. The soldiers used to cheer it, and Scammon liked that.

Scammon's importance could not be tut-tutted; and it was with a good deal of relief that the men observed that this dog did not show jealousy of the young beaver—paid, in fact, almost no attention to it.

They lost a canoe, smashed against a rock, but managed

to save most of the supplies it had contained. Nobody was hurt.

They thought for a while that they had lost another man through desertion. Private George Shannon, who had been told off to watch the two horses on the bank, was missing— as were the horses. After two weeks—from August 26 to September 11—he showed up, barely alive, having run out of cartridges and been obliged to live on berries. He had supposed that the company was *ahead* of him, when in truth it was *behind*, and he had raced along the bank in pursuit. At last he had given up, and had turned back with the wild idea of making his way to St. Louis alone, perhaps eating the horse as he went; for he had lost one horse.

They saw many buffalo, but at a distance, mostly to the northeast. Sometimes these extended in black herds as far as the eye could see. Captain Clark, who had perched himself on an eminence for this purpose, reckoned that in one afternoon he had seen ten thousand of them.

They saw their first prairie dogs—the French called them *petits chiens*—September 7, a Friday. They were enchanted by the pert little animals that sat up before their holes. They tried for hours to flush them out, pouring many barrels of water down various holes, but the best they could get was one small drowned one. They saved the pelt and skeleton of this, to be sent to the President.

The river could be very rough, and it was shallower now. One day, because of shoal water and sandbars, they made only four miles.

Discipline was better, though there was to be one further flare-up. Private John Newman was insolent to Captain Lewis, and a court martial sentenced him to seventy-five lashes. When they learned what was about to be done, some visiting Oto chiefs protested. That, they said by means of sign language, would be cruel. It would be savage, degrading. They themselves never beat anybody, even their own children, nor did any other Indians. They might burn a captive to death over a slow fire, but that was a test of his courage and should make him proud; and besides, it had always been done that way. The thought of *whipping* a man shocked them. Nevertheless, Newman was lashed, the Otos shaking their heads.

The steady southeast breeze had shifted to due south, and the nights were getting colder, but the mosquitoes were as bad as ever.

Pierre Cruzatte, an *engagé*, was blind in one eye and nearsighted in the other, yet he was an expert boatman. And he was more. He was a fiddler of note, and he had his fiddle with him. More than once, after a wearying day, he had entertained the men in camp. Now he was asked to entertain some Oto and Missouri chiefs in a powwow called by the captains on the west bank of the river.[14]

The meeting itself must have been a bore. They smoked, passing the pipe around, and they grunted and talked interminably. They never laughed, for it was a grave occasion. Captain Lewis told them at great length of the change in the Great White Fathers, and assured them—slowly, to give the interpreters a chance—that the United States would take care of all their needs, provided they behaved themselves; and they listened to this, solemnly bowing their heads, and then smoked some more.

Afterward, however, there was dancing to the music of Cruzatte's violin, and the Indians hugely enjoyed this, though they did not participate. One of the soldiers, a sergeant named John Floyd, danced so hard that he overheated himself, and that night he came down with a fever. Captain Clark was to record it as "a bilious colic." It might have been appendicitis. At any rate, and for all their medication, or perhaps because of it, he died the next day. They named the place where they buried him Floyd Bluff.[15]

This was their first death, and it saddened them, but it did not deter them. The men at large picked, to succeed Floyd as sergeant, three possible successors, all of whom were acceptable to both captains, and then they all voted: Patrick Gass, another diarist, was elected. He stood only five feet seven, and was bushy-bearded and barrel-chested, an Irishman from Pennsylvania, a professional soldier, and, incidentally, a carpenter. Now it was *Sergeant* Gass.

Thus everything was proceeding smoothly—until they met the Sioux.

CHAPTER

6

Confrontation on a Riverbank

THE VERY WORD SIOUX (a shortening of the Ojibwa *Nadowessioux*) meant "enemy." In the sign language that was understood over most of the upper Mississippi–Missouri country, the motion for it was a forefinger swiftly drawn across the Adam's apple.

The first ones, though, were easy: they were almost a disappointment. They were Yanktons, members of a minor Siouan tribe and not at all belligerent. Placidly they consented to accept the white men's gifts, and to sip whatever of his whiskey they managed to get; and placidly, nodding approval—though they probably did not understand a word of it—they listened to Captain Lewis's palaver about the *new* Great White Father and the need for an end to the wars among his children. They were embarrassingly mild. They didn't even scowl.

It was different with the Tetons. These too were Sioux, and they too sought gifts shamelessly, but they were disagreeable about it. Moreover, they were much more numerous than had been the Yanktons.

They were soon coming to the riverbank from their villages, which were far back from the Missouri, and they were not an attractive lot. They wore hawks' feathers in their hair, and their faces were daubed with grease. Most of the men carried bows and arrows. A few had muskets, but these were weapons with faulty locks, which the Indians could not repair, or with worn-out flints, which they could not replace, weapons that French and British traders had willingly given away, and they were carried rather for show, for prestige purposes, than as a threat. The Lewis-Clark men had rifles, guns that would carry twice as far as any musket and with much greater accuracy. The rifle took longer to reload, and for this reason the musket was still preferred by some soldiers as a more reliable arm in battle, especially when fitted with a bayonet; but in this changeover period the rifle was by far the superior weapon for scouting, and in the woods or the wilderness. The Indians knew this.

The explorers had, in addition, one large and two small swivel guns. These were mounted amidships of the keelboat, ready to be fired in any direction. It is not likely that the Teton Sioux or any other Indians in that part of the world ever before had seen a swivel gun, a sort of light cannon loaded with grape, but they could easily guess what these were.

They were not fazed. They stood along the shore, silent, glowering at the keelboat and the tied-alongside canoes. By the time Captain Lewis's interpreter-messenger had made arrangements for a proper powwow there must have been almost a thousand of them, including the squaws and the children, and more were appearing all the time.

Lewis and Clark went ashore.

They were handicapped from the beginning in the matter of communication. Pierre Dorian, who would have been a perfect interpreter, was not with them, for he had gone to a nearby village to visit his son, a half-breed trader. They were obliged to depend upon two of the *engagés*, who not only had a scanty knowledge of the Teton dialect but were not even very learned in the sign language. Still, the powwow would, in any event, have failed. The red men were not interested in words, even if these had been accurately transmitted. They were interested only in presents, expensive presents, and plenty of them. Never before had they dealt with military men, but only with merchants. Never before had they met men who refused to be mulcted.

Most of the chiefs remained impassive as Lewis stumbled through his Great White Father speech, but that was to be expected. The younger men, however, the hotheads who had not yet hacked off their first scalps, were restless. They frowned. Some of them strung their bows, and a few even fished arrows out of their quivers.

When Lewis was finished he distributed the usual gifts —medals, beads, mirrors, and a splendid army officer's coat for the Number One chief, a personage by the name of Black Buffalo Bull. But this was not enough, as the chiefs themselves bluntly insisted.

They wanted tobacco: their own tobacco was horrid. They wanted whiskey. As far as the explorers could gather, they wanted just about everything in the expedition. Sometimes they blustered, sometimes they wheedled, telling about how poor they were. Lewis and Clark said no, and since they saw that the formal confab was getting nowhere they retreated to the keelboat. They took with them four of the chief chiefs, including Black Buffalo Bull and one named The Partisan, a troublemaker against whom they had been warned by Dorian and his fellow French fur merchants. *Why* they thus honored The Partisan is not clear. Perhaps they were afraid to leave him behind? The young warriors were still fingering their bows, still muttering. The Partisan,

SIOUX TENTS ALONG THE MISSOURI

left with them, might have organized a massacre.

The four chiefs, aboard, were given a quarter of a glass of whiskey apiece and showed over the homely grandeurs of the boat, which never did have a name. They were duly impressed, but when it came time to go ashore they demurred. The Partisan in particular pretended to be drunk—he could not possibly have been drunk on so little—and made a fuss about staying.

At last they were got ashore, in charge of Captain Clark, who immediately had further troubles.

Black Buffalo Bull and the others again and again had urged the white men to stay over in their own Siouan villages for at least a few days, and Clark and Lewis again and again had pointed out that already it was late September—this was the 25th—and that if they expected to make the shelter of the Mandan villages before the snow flew and the first of the ice came whirling down the river they could not afford to visit.

Now this plea was resumed, rather more roughly. Two of the younger braves on the shore seized the canoe's painter and refused to release it. The Partisan, still stupidly pretending to be drunk, threw his arms around the mast and hugged it.

Furious, William Clark drew his sword.

The murmurs died, and the silence was ominous. More bows were strung, more arrows drawn from quivers. The soldiers lowered the muzzles of their rifles. The air fairly tingled with electricity.

None of this was lost on Meriwether Lewis, who watched from the keelboat anchored nearby. He sensed, even at that distance, that here was the moment of truth. If one young brave let fly an arrow, if any soldier gripped his gun too tightly so that it went off, the result would be a slaughter. The Americans might not lose many men; they might win the immediate battle; but after such a fight they could not possibly press on up the Missouri. The Teton Sioux would summon all their kin, and a first-class war would be on. That would end the expedition, a failure.

On the other hand, any sign of retreat, of nervousness, would be pounced upon by the wily Sioux, who sought just that. Thank God, Clark was standing firm!

Lewis thought fast. He ordered all three of the swivel guns to be loaded and manned and pointed in the direction of the shore. The two smaller ones were loaded with buckshot, the large one with sixteen one-and-a-half-ounce balls. Fired over the heads of Clark and his men, they could have done ghastly damage to the crowded Indians.

At the same time Lewis sent the second canoe ashore filled with soldiers, their rifles loaded and cocked.

It worked.

Black Buffalo Bull commanded the young braves to drop the painter of the canoe, and they obeyed. The Partisan was prised loose from the mast. Looks were angry enough; words were harsh; but no shot was fired, no arrow flew.

It had been an extremely close thing, and when they encamped that night on an island a few miles upstream they were still tense, short, taut. The previous night they had pitched camp on a similar island, which they named Good-Humored Island because they had all been in such high spirits at the time, but *this* island they named *Bad*-Humored Island.[16]

Next morning there were red men along both banks, red men who cajoled, wheedled, begged for tobacco, offered their squaws. Had they summoned cousins from far places, and were they stalling for time?

The visitors did stay in those parts longer than they had meant to do, but this was only because they lost their anchor in a boating accident and failed, after much dragging, to recover it. They improvised an anchor out of rocks, and went determinedly upstream.

There was one further attempt at a powwow, but, though the Indians appeared to be conciliatory, the absence of a capable interpreter again made any real understanding impossible. Not for an instant did the explorers let down their guard. The swivel guns were manned night and day; the sentries, as always, were stringent; and nobody got much sleep.

For four days the Sioux trudged along the banks, calling out in supplication, but at last they quit.

The word undoubtedly had gone out that these new white men were not like the previous ones. They would not be bullied or browbeaten.

In consequence they were treated with respect by the next Indians they encountered. These were the Arikaras, a Siouan tribe but naturally friendly, intelligent, amiable. The customary gifts were distributed among them, and they seemed satisfied and even grateful. Lewis made his usual speech, which was politely received.

Two things in particular marked the Arikaras apart from any other Indians yet encountered.

Instead of tepees made of sleazy hides or the flimsy bark huts or hogans that were usual among red men, the Arikaras built conical lodges made of willow wattles covered with straw and cemented with six or seven inches of mud. These were handsome; and they were large, some of them as much as fifty feet in diameter. They were kept clean. They were laid out neatly, according to a plan, with clean wide streets between them.

In addition—and this was even more extraordinary— the Arikaras did not like liquor. It made them act foolish, they explained, and they would consent to drink it only if they were paid to. If the white man wanted a show, an entertainment, the Arikaras argued, he should be prepared to pay for it.

The Arikaras, by nature a peaceful people,[17] were, as Sioux, automatically if not very enthusiastically at war with the Mandans, the next tribe upriver. Lewis asked them to make peace, as they were willing to do, the more so because his bravura treatment of the terrible Tetons had made a deep impression upon them.

The Tetons were still to be considered, to be guarded against. They would be around all winter, and they had many relatives. Even before he encountered them, Meriwether Lewis had decided that he would not send the keelboat back to St. Louis with letters and specimens until the following spring. He had previously planned to send it in the fall, but now he feared to weaken the force that he would have in winter quarters in or near the Mandan villages. The near-thing with the Teton Sioux undoubtedly had strengthened this resolve.

Already white gulls and brant could be seen flying south. Soon the snows would begin, and the river would be clogged with ice.

They pushed on up for the Mandans.

They had a special interest in the Mandans.

7

The Mystery of Prince Madoc

THERE WAS A KING OF NORTH WALES many years ago, and his name was Owain Gwyneth, and when he died—it was in 1169—things more or less fell apart, so that a state of anarchy existed. This discouraged the youngest of his sons, the Prince Madoc, who, in order to get away from the turmoil, took a ship out on the ocean—or ten ships, or twelve—heading west. He was never heard of again—not, at least, at home.

The tale tells that Madoc reached America. He might have heard that one Leif Ericson had discovered a land he called Vineland out in that direction, or he might simply have been looking for some place in which he could get away from it all. At any rate his followers, fastidious fellows, stoutly refused to mix with the crude aborigines, and instead interbred among themselves and flourished until they numbered, it was said at one time, more than five thousand.

They were bearded, and very blond. All descriptions of them insist upon the exceeding lightness of their skin and the yellowness of their hair, which is odd because the Welsh in general are a swarthy race with brunettes predominating among them.

They had lost their culture but they clung to their language, which nobody tried to take away from them.

There are many versions of what happened to the Madogwys. One has it that a branch of them split off from the main body and went south to Mexico, where they founded the Aztec empire. Another declares that they persisted as Christians and that indeed their most venerated relic was the Bible Madoc had brought with him; and *this* is *very* odd because that crossing was made some 300 years before Gutenberg invented the printed press and more than 400 years before the Good Book was translated into Welsh.

These Christian Madocians, one story has it, were almost wiped out by their enemies in a great battle fought near the falls of the Ohio,[18] and they survived as only a small, weak remnant of the original band, always on the move, still, however, resolutely speaking Welsh.

Yet another version of the Madoc myth has the group somehow merged with the Jaredites, one of the lost tribes of Israel, who were scattered in another great battle, near Palmyra, New York. A survivor of that battle, the angel Mormon, recorded the event in a book made of solid gold, a book Joseph Smith was to dig up many years later. Smith mislaid the original, but not before he had made a copy, and this was to become the foundation of a religious cult known officially as the Church of the Latter-Day Saints, and to the general public as the Mormons. It is not recorded whether the original Madocians practiced polygamy.

One thing only about the Madocians was certain: they were to be found over the horizon. They never quite got into sight. Rumors of such a people there assuredly were, and in great numbers, but the people themselves always seemed to keep out of the way. They were elusive. As the frontier in America moved west they moved west just ahead of it.

The legend of Prince Madoc had come to America with the first Welsh settlers a little before the outbreak of the Revolution, and at the time that Lewis and Clark were about to start on their momentous expedition it was at its height, enjoying a sudden, unexpected, and unaccountable popularity. Robert Southey was writing a long poem entitled "Madoc." A clergyman who passionately believed in its truth had just published a best-selling book about Madoc and his tribe. Welshmen all over the world, wherever two or three were gathered together, could talk of little else. Prince Madoc was the glory of their nation, embodying in his person as in the history of his followers all that was clean and noble and good about that people, a breath of fresh air from the olden days blown into this stale modern world. Prince Madoc was, somehow, Rousseau's Noble Savage. He was the Nature Boy of the Western World, a creature of naïve but admirable imagination.

Various Indian tribes from time to time had been identified with the Madocians, but when they were approached, when they were actually glimpsed, actually met, it turned out to be otherwise. Always it was some different tribe, some tribe a little farther west. There were the Tuscaroras, the Cherokees, the Paducahs, the Omans, the Osage, the Creeks, the Navajo, the Hopi, the Modoc, the Mandans, the Doegs, the Shawnees, and others.

When the word got out that the exploring captains meant to pass a whole winter among the Mandans of the northernmost stretches of the Great Muddy, excitement must have been intense among the true believers, the Welsh in America and in Wales, for the Mandans, it was currently being related, *were,* for sure, the original wandering Welshmen. Soon the world would know.

A decade earlier the question had seemed for a little while to be answered. A young Welshman, John Evans, had come to America from his native land, backed by friends

who had specifically charged him to seek out the Madogwys,
the descendants of Prince Madoc and his people.

Evans was operating on a shoestring, and he spent more
than a year in the eastern part of the new republic, trying,
not very successfully, to raise money from the American
Welsh. At last he made his way to St. Louis, Spanish territory
then, where he began to ask all sorts of questions. The
Spaniards, suspicious, taking him for a spy, threw him into
jail.

The Spaniards at just that time were not worried about
the French, who had been weakened by war, nor were they
worried about the infant United States, but they were decidedly worried about the British in western and central
Canada, who tended to seep down into the Louisiana country. The Spaniards wanted all that land for themselves, and
believed that they were entitled to it. They hoped that some
day, when they were strong enough, they could open Louisiana clear over to the Pacific Ocean. They were leery of
British traders.

How long they kept John Evans in jail is not known, but
it is virtually certain that they released him at last only after
he had pledged himself to work for them. Since the incarcera-
tion Spain and Great Britain had declared war, so John
Evans, by doing this, was guilty of treason; and it was certain
that he could not go home again.

The Spaniards sent Evans up the Missouri, with orders
to seek out the Mandans and report on them. If these Indians
really *were* Welsh in their origin, that would strengthen Great
Britain's rather shadowy claim to the northern part of the
Louisiana territory.

Evans spent seven months among the Mandans, and
came back to report that they were *not* Welsh. However,
since this was obviously what the Spaniards had wished him
to report, and since he was in their power, his asseveration

was looked upon askance. This disbelief was strengthened by the circumstance that John Evans soon after his return had taken to drink and was known as a man who would do anything for a bottle. He died in New Orleans late in May of 1799. He was only twenty-nine.

The question, then, was still unanswered.

Among the many grave responsibilities with which the captains were saddled, this was perhaps the most easily borne. Indeed, it could be that they never knew about it. Certainly they made no mention of it in their joint journal.

The Mandans undeniably *were* lighter than most full-blooded Indians, lighter by far than any Indians any member of the expedition ever had seen before; but by no stretch of imagination could they be called white. They *did* have some jawbreaking names—Clark and his companion were soon to grow accustomed to chatting with such minor sachems as Mahpahpapapassato (Horned Weasel), Matocoquepa (Second Bear), Tartongawaka (Buffalo Medicine), and Keetooshsahawha (Place of the Many Beaver)—but they were not bearded, and most emphatically they were not blond.

It was among the Mandans that the travelers first glimpsed the coracle, a craft then peculiar to this people.

There were no birchbark canoes in that part of the world because there were no birches. The canoes were usually dugouts, eight to ten feet long, each holding three persons, a bow paddle, a middle paddle, and in the stern a sweep. These were clumsy but strong, and they could not be sunk. Two or more of them lashed together with trees might form a raft suitable for heavy hauling.

The coracle was something different, a light, ludicrous craft, used in fishing and for getting back and forth across the river from one village to another, but seldom used for any sort of long haul. Each was an openwork basket made

MANDAN WOMEN

of willow sticks held together with strips of green rawhide and covered by a whole buffalo hide, the hairy side out. There was always plenty of buffalo hide. When the Mandans went out to hunt buffalo they sometimes left tons of meat behind on the plain, being ill equipped to cart it all; but they never failed to skin out the beasts and to take home the hides.

Cowhide could be used, but buffalo hide was preferred.

The coracle was either perfectly round or slightly oval: a typical one might measure five feet by three and a half feet across the top. The bottom was round.

These *looked* tippy—they looked like large untidy eggshells—but in fact they were most marvelously steady, and there was not much that the capricious Missouri could do to them.

The paddler—the coracle was about three feet deep—stood in the exact middle. She held the paddle before her and drew it toward her for each stroke, describing a figure eight. The paddle, wooden, was about five feet or a little longer. The paddler always was a squaw. No man would be seen operating one.

An amazing amount of cargo could be loaded into a coracle, yet the thing drew only a few inches of water. When a portage was reached or some other overground journey faced, the craft, weighing only twenty to thirty pounds, could be emptied, upended, and carried across the back by means of a headband. This too, of course, was done by the squaws.

The significance of the coracles on the upper Missouri —a significance lost upon the members of the Lewis-Clark expedition—lay in the fact that they were not to be found anywhere else in the world except Wales. Madocians were to be quick to seize upon this as a proof that the Mandans were descendants of the original Madogwys, or Madawgwys.

The fact was that the coracle, under one name or another, had been known and used for centuries, and only recently had been discarded for more convenient boats. The ancient Egyptians had them, and so had the ancient Britons, and the Irish, who called them curraghs. But it is true that no other tribe of American Indians ever seemed to have used any form of the coracle, and it is also true that at this time, early in the nineteenth century, the coracle in the popular mind was associated with Wales, where, and especially on the rivers Teifi and Wye, they were still common sights.

Moreover—and this too the visitors did not know, though much was to be made of it later—there is a conceivable linguistic link. The Mandans called the coracle a *koorig*. In Welsh the word is *corwg* (pronounced corrug). The paddle, in the language of the Mandans, was *ree;* in Welsh it is *rhwyf* (pronounced reef).

The visitors called them bullboats, and found them comical. Set a whole batch of squaws to crossing the river, each in her own coracle, and if the water was rough, as so often it was,[19] the boats themselves would be out of sight most of the time, while the women's heads bobbed up and down like so many crazy, dusky mermaids. This was always good for a laugh.

The Noble Savage, then, had not yet been isolated. He must still be somewhere farther west, just a little beyond the horizon.

The Lewis-Clark people were to bring back many curious specimens, but these did not include the descendants of Prince Madoc.

CHAPTER

8

When the Snow Began to Fly

THE MANDANS WERE AMIABLE, but they were not strong. They numbered barely three hundred and fifty braves,[20] and though they could count on about eighty Omahas and some six hundred Minnetaras as allies, they were almost completely surrounded by Sioux, who did not wish them well. Small wonder that they welcomed the whites, knowing that these would stay all winter.

The Mandans occupied five villages, high up near the mouth of the Knife River, where the up-Missouri, which until this time had been headed mostly north, makes a great swing to the west.[21] Adjacent to these villages, though not located inside any one of them, and far enough back from the banks of the Big Muddy so that they would not have to fear a spring spate—about a mile and a half—the explorers built Fort Mandan.

It was a triangular structure, open on top, the two long faces measuring eighteen feet on the outside, the third face little more than a gate. It was made almost entirely of cottonwood logs notched at the ends and "dobbed" together

75

with mud at the cracks. The fireplaces, however, were of fieldstone. They traveled far afield to get that stone.

This was called a fort only because it was a United States Army post. It had no moat, no crenellated parapet, no bastion or scarp or glacis, no machicolation. Any European military engineer would have laughed at the thing, which would not have withstood an artillery attack for an hour, no matter how small the pieces. But its eight-foot walls would have stopped a Sioux onset. The Clark and Lewis men still did not trust the Sioux,[22] whom they took to be poor losers.

They did not entirely trust the Mandans either. For example, and though this made for some hard feeling, they would not allow any of the villagers to remain inside the walls of the fort after sunset.

The Mandans' own houses were similar in construction to those of the Arikaras—large, oval, strong—and their streets were clean.

Diplomatically, the visitors refused to recognize any single, over-all chief. Instead, they selected the oldest and most respected chief in each village and honored him with the same gifts that each of the others got.

Beads and buckles and brightly colored ribbons were gifts enough for the ordinary braves, though what the braves really craved and what they begged for was whiskey, which the captains conscientiously withheld; but for the top chiefs coats were due—coats as polychromatic as Joseph's own, and equipped, in addition, with gold epaulettes, with sword belts, with all manner of froggery and scrambled eggs.[23]

The captains had with them any number of bright-colored beads, and when they left the East they had no fewer than fifteen *dozen* pewter looking-glasses; but looking glasses and beads were not enough for the high chiefs, who were given medals, of which there were three classes, besides the coats and brightly plumed hats.

There seemed to be an inordinate number of chiefs. There were times when it looked as though every male above the age of twenty so described himself; and the captains could not call the claims to question, for fear of hurting important feelings.

Tobacco was always welcome. Even before the visitors had learned the language they were called upon to squat and smoke solemnly for long periods of time. The Indians supplied the pipes.

Cruzatte and his fiddle were in demand. These red men had no music. Their dances were done to the beat of crude tom-toms and to the dancers' and spectators' *hup-hup-hup-hup*. They loved to watch the white men dancing together, their arms around one another, the "follower," playing a woman, always with a kerchief tied around his left arm.[24]

The captains had a Harrison air gun, a device recently invented in England, where poaching was widely practiced, and popular there, though scarcely known in the United States. They had brought this along, it would seem, largely for their own amusement; but it proved to be even more amusing to the Indians, who marveled to see birds brought down with no more than a muffled *pfft*.

The gristmill, an accepted necessity to the white men, thrilled the Indians, who gasped to see the speed with which it transformed maize and wheat into powder. *They*, of course, had always used two flat stones.

There were two blacksmiths in the company, and when the fort was finished and the explorers had settled down for the winter they untarpaulined a portable forge in the very middle of the keelboat. This filled their hosts with amazement. The bellows frightened them just at first, and always fascinated them. They voted it "big medicine." They would squat before it for hours, gawping.

Incomparably the biggest attraction, however, was York.

No Negro ever before had been seen, or even heard of, in that part of the world. York drew crowds wherever he went; and he loved it.

He was a young man, husky, dark. Clark had inherited him from his father, John, in a will dated July 24, 1799. In his journal Captain Clark habitually referred to him as "my black Servent": but he was undoubtedly a slave.

Word of this phenomenon sped ahead of the party, and each new group of Mandans they encountered on their way to the villages that comprised the heart of the tribe demanded, first off, to see York. They would do this even before they began to whine for whiskey. Some believed him to be a wild beast that had somehow been domesticated, and York played up to this belief, snorting ominously, baring his teeth, rolling his eyes. Others believed that he was really a white man, painted, for some strange reason, black. Not infrequently a daring brave would spit on his thumb and rub York's arm or leg in an attempt to get the paint off.

York's hair was his biggest attraction. When he uncovered, a gasp would go up. For letting a redskin run his hands through that crinkly black stuff he could get almost any price—a squaw, for instance, if need be, though York never was to be short of squaws.

The Mandans were woefully slack in matters of sex.[25] They passed their women around like biscuits, and actually *urged* York to sleep with them. They were eager, afterward, to learn the details. York, a good-natured man, didn't mind. He was to have busy nights all that winter. As far as he was concerned, the expedition already was a success.

This was buffalo country. Elk, deer, bear, and beaver they had in plenty, but the mainstay of the Mandans was the bison, not only as food but also because of its hide. When they had enough horses—their neighbors were industrious horse thieves—they would hunt in a pack, shooting down the

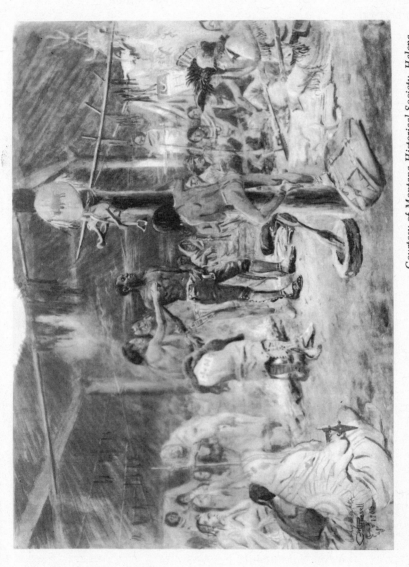

CHARLES M. RUSSELL'S PAINTING OF THE NEGRO YORK AMONG THE MANDANS

beasts from behind as they ran. At other times they used a decoy, an agile young Indian who was wrapped in a buffalo robe and held a buffalo head on the end of a stick. This courageous lad—he ran an excellent chance of being trampled to death—would find for himself a rocky hiding place near some steep bluff, and crouch there, waiting for the rest of the braves, on horseback and on foot, to steer a herd of buffalo in his direction. When they were close enough he would rise and lead them running toward the precipice; if he was lucky he would duck into his hiding place just before the thundering herd engulfed him.

The stupid beasts, heads lowered, would plunge right over the edge. It never seemed to occur to the ones in the rear to wonder where those in the front had gone. They ran on—to their death—by the scores, sometimes by the hundreds. A few, crippled, might manage to limp away. Most of them were slaughtered where they lay, and skinned out. These places, in the nature of them, always were a long distance from the villages, and the Mandans, still living in the Stone Age, had not invented or been given the wheel, so that most of the carcasses had to be abandoned. The choicest chunks of meat—always the hump, the most desirable part—would be hauled away. The rest, perhaps nine-tenths of the whole, would be left for the wolves.

The stuff could be smoked, and one hunt might net a family man enough to last all the winter through. He was entitled to whatever he could carry or drag. A single man, however, was expected to share with his neighbors, if it so happened that they were in need. He would not be *asked* for meat, outright. Instead, a squaw from some nearby lodge, saying nothing, would squat by the door of the bachelor's lodge until at last the bachelor "understands the hint and gives her gratuitously a part for her family." [26]

The snow began to fly October 21, a Sunday. There

were seven inches of it that night.

On November 13, by which time the explorers were comfortably snuggled into Fort Mandan, the first ice came floating down the river.

Late that same month a party of Tetons jumped a party of Mandans out on the plain, and killed one of them and stole all their horses. When the news of this reached Fort Mandan, William Clark offered to raise a force of volunteers and lead a punishment party against the Tetons. The offer was declined; but it undoubtedly raised Clark in the esteem of his hosts. It was explained that the winter already was too far advanced to risk such a party, which might never get back.

Truly, it was colder. The night of December 16–17, at sunrise, the captains recorded 45 degrees below zero Fahrenheit. On such nights the sentinel had to be relieved every half hour, for fear of frozen feet. Even the Indians, who seemed to be made of iron, sometimes got frostbitten.

The chiefs and their squaws were in the habit of dropping in at Fort Mandan for a pipe and a few words of gossip, a custom the captains encouraged because it helped them to learn the language and to gather information about the countryside, and especially the country to the west; but they asked the Indians not to come on Christmas Day and New Year's Day, explaining that these were big medicine days for them. In truth, there was little enough by the way of celebration. They paraded, and they fired a *feu de joie,* and each man was allotted a tot of whiskey, and that was about all.

January 15, from midnight to three A.M. there was a complete eclipse of the moon, which the captains were able accurately to predict; but this did not seem to impress the red men.

The captains busied themselves with writing their journal from field notes, keeping records of temperatures and of ice movements in the river, preparing a dictionary of the Mandan tongue, and collecting specimens and mounting these for President Jefferson and for Henry Dearborn, the Secretary of War—five boxes of stuffed prairie dogs, magpies, a prairie hen, much else, besides rock and soil samples, and some of Captain Clark's maps. Captain Lewis wrote a long letter to the President:

". . . These have been forwarded with a view of their being presented to the Philosophical society of Philadelphia, in order that they may under their direction be examined or analyzed. After examining these specimens yourself, I would thank you to have a copy of their labels made out, and retained untill my return. . . . I have transmitted to the Secretary at War, every information relative to the geography of the country which we possess, together with a view of the Indian nations, containing information relative to them, on those points with which, I conceived it important that the government should be informed. . . . Since our arrival at this place we have subsisted principally on meat, with which our guns have supplyed us amply, and have thus been enabled to reserve the parched meal, portable soup, and a considerable proportion of pork and flour, which we had intended for the more difficult parts of our voyage. . . . We do not calculate on completeing our voyage within the present year, but expect to reach the Pacific Ocean, and return, as far as the head of the Missouri, or perhaps to this place before winter. You may therefore expect me to meet you at Montachello in September 1806." [27]

About the middle of February they began to work on the boats, extricating them from the ice. The river to the west, they had been told, was narrower, shallower, rockier, and at least as squirmy as the river they had until this time known. The keelboat, the plan was, would be sent back to

St. Louis as soon as conditions permitted. The pirogues, after repair, would be supplemented by six somewhat smaller dugout canoes. The men began to build those canoes. They had only cottonwood to work with, not a material they would have chosen, but they wanted to be ready when the time came, when the way was clear.

March 3 a flock of ducks passed up the river.

There were repeated rumors that the Sioux were preparing to go on the warpath. Then came reports that already they were practicing on their neighbors: they had beset upon and killed most of a party of fifty Assiniboins north of the Mandan villages, and undoubtedly when the weather permitted they would strive to block the farther advance of the white men.

March 23 the villages had their first rain, which cleared away most of the snow.

Rifles were cleaned and their locks regulated. The swivel guns were put in order. Provisions were inspected. Blankets were aired.

It had been a long winter and a hard one, but the end was in sight.

The men brightened as the day of departure approached; but at this time, not unexpectedly, Toussaint Charbonneau began to make trouble.

He was a barge of a man, French, with a high opinion of his own value. He had been hired in St. Louis as an interpreter, this being a special rank created for him and for the other interpreter, Drewer; they got $25 a month apiece, as compared with the $5 a month for privates, $8 for sergeants. Now Charbonneau blusteringly demanded that before he went on, went west, it must be promised that he would be relieved of the usual daily humdrum duties on the river as well as in camp.

He had picked a bad time for this. Drewer, who was also

French, had done a great deal of hunting, at which he was very skillful; but Charbonneau was purely and simply an interpreter, and now that the expedition was about to pass into the far western district where no Siouan dialect was spoken, and no French, his usefulness would seem to be at an end. Captain Lewis reminded him of this and suggested that he be honorably discharged. Abashed, Charbonneau retreated.

He was soon back. All right, he would consent to work just like the other men, but there was one stipulation: he must be allowed to bring his wife and child.

The child was a baby, born in the fort on February 11. The mother was named Sacajawea, which means Bird-Woman. She was a mere girl, really, and the infant was her first baby. Before its birth, and fearful of having a hard labor, she had appealed to Charbonneau, who in turn appealed to Captain Lewis. Could he have some of the snake rattle? Lewis was in charge of the medicine chest, which included Dr. Rush's pills, a large supply of mercury for the treatment of syphilis, with which it was known that the Indians were rotten, and of course the nether ends of some rattlesnakes, since it was common knowledge that this stuff, ground into a powder, was a sure antidote against snake venom. Somebody had told Charbonneau that it was equally efficacious when used to ease a woman's labor, especially if it was to be a first baby. Lewis had never heard of this, but he was willing to take a chance, and he gave Charbonneau some of the rattle, which Charbonneau ground up and put into a mug of water and gave to Sacajawea. Within ten minutes her labor pains began, and they were extremely short, without complications. The baby was a boy. They named him Baptiste.

The idea of taking a woman along on such a trip would have been unthinkable except for one circumstance.

Sacajawea was a Snake, and so she spoke Shoshonean.

She had been captured as a child in a remote clash on the plains, and she had never forgotten her native tongue. She was probably the only person for a thousand miles around who could make head or tail of it, and on the Missouri she had picked up the Mandan dialect of the Siouan language, so that *she* could act as an interpreter, a badly needed one, in the Shoshone country.

Lewis of course concurred. Probably nobody even thought to ask Sacajawea whether she was willing to make the trek, nursing a baby all the while. Indian women were expected to do as they were told. Demurrance was not tolerated.

So it was that when, on April 7, the keelboat was started down the river with six United States Army privates and a corporal, President Jefferson's specimens, and three French traders (one of whom was to act as pilot), and the eight canoes started soon afterward from Fort Mandan for the upper Missouri, the utterly unknown country, the latter craft contained thirty-three persons in addition to a babe in arms.

It was five o'clock in the afternoon of a cool, clear day.

9

Which Way to Turn?

THE RIVER UNTIL NOW had been cruel, true; but such mild cruelty would have been positively welcomed in the *upper* river. Time and again they had to get out and push, often up to their armpits in water that was as cold as ice. The bottom was sometimes mud, sometimes sharp stones that cut through the soles of their moccasins: their boots had long since been worn out. They had foiled the Sioux by leaving so early, but they did not know this and more than once must have wished that they had lingered a little longer in the Mandan villages.

The morning of May 2 it snowed heavily from dawn until ten o'clock, and at other times there was a great deal of cold, biting rain, rain that was all daggers. Once there was a hailstorm, by far the worst that any of them ever had known: they measured one stone at seven inches across. The rattlesnakes were somewhat smaller than those in the East, but just as venomous. The grizzly bears were even bigger and more ferocious. The river itself—the Indian word for it meant troubled waters—was as cantankerous as before. There

were as many mosquitoes at night; and in addition there
was a new pest, in the daytime, a sort of blowfly they called
the buffalo gnat and that annoyed their eyes.

Previously they had at least enjoyed plenty of fuel, but
now they had only cottonwood, punky stuff, until they
learned to utilize the dried buffalo droppings that they called
chips or bodewash.[28] These stank, but they did the trick,
and there were always hundreds of them near at hand.

May 15 there was a sudden squall, and one of the large
pirogues heeled over, spilling most of its contents. At the
helm was Charbonneau, one of the worst boatmen of the
expedition, and he was, literally, scared stiff. He could not
swim. He did nothing to try to right the boat, which had
been prevented from capsizing only by its sail, and he did
not touch the steering sweep until Cruzatte in the bow
pointed a rifle at him and threatened to shoot unless he did
his part. Charbonneau's wife, on the other hand, the Bird-
Woman, Sacajawea, who had been seated amidships with
the papoose strapped on her back, without a word started
to scoop out of the water such floating objects as she could
reach.[29]

This pirogue, as it happened, contained most of the expedition's papers and almost all its instruments, besides the
medical supplies. Only a few were lost, but it was a near
thing for a few minutes there, and when the pirogue at last
did make the bank she was awash almost to the gunwales.
Lewis, several hundred yards away, had whipped off his
coat, but he did not jump in, which was just as well, for he
probably would have been drowned, the river being in one
of its rages at the moment.

Had that pirogue completely collapsed, the expedition
would have been obliged to turn back.

Until this time there had been no trouble about drink-
ing water. The men had simply reached over the side and

scooped up a palmful any time they felt thirsty. Now, however, there was suddenly a great deal of diarrhea and dysentery. The water, which tasted bitter, was acting as a strong purgative. Lewis believed that the cause of this was alkali held in the sand swept down from tributaries, and he ordered the men to let the water stand a little while, to permit the sand to settle, before they drank. Evidently he was right; for the trouble ceased.

April 26 they passed the mouth of the Yellowstone, a large river. May 29 they discovered a river that Clark named after a girl friend, Julia Hancock, who was only thirteen years old at the time.[30] June 4 they came to a tremendous fork.

Which was the Missouri?

The river on the right, extending northward, *looked* more like the Missouri, being muddy, and it was slightly wider than the river on the left, 362 yards to 200 yards. The men all voted for the river on the right; but the captains had their doubts.

The more southerly river was clear and had a clean stony bottom, which suggested that it had come from the faraway mountains, the mountains they must surmount before they could reach the Pacific Ocean, whereas the northward-extending river, being muddy, might have meandered for many miles through flat country, prairie country.

They pitched camp while they thought it over. They sent small bodies of men, each headed by a sergeant, a few miles up the north river, a few miles up the south, but these trips were inconclusive, indicating nothing. They must go themselves, the captains knew. The fate of the whole expedition would hang upon this. Should they take the wrong turning, by the time they had discovered their mistake it would be too late to rectify it, for winter would be almost upon them and the only thing left for them to do would be to hurry back to the Mandan villages while they could still

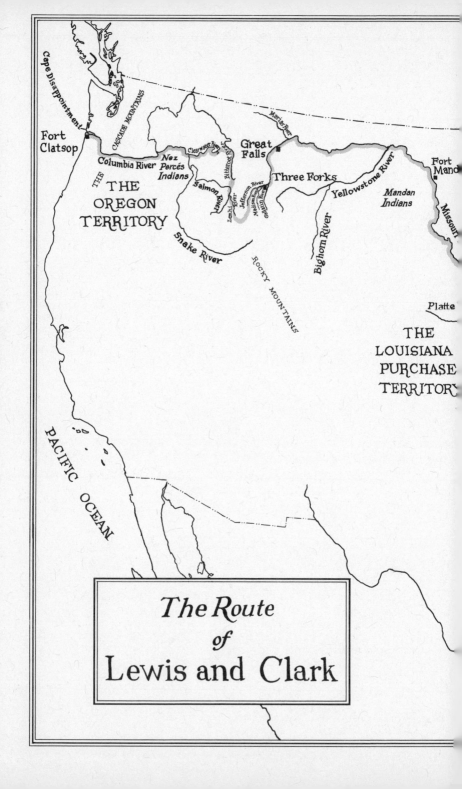

The Route
of
Lewis and Clark

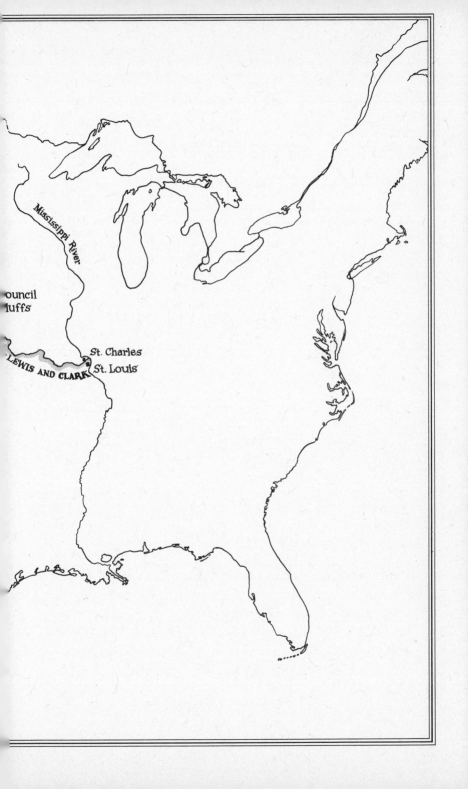

get there. Then, in the spring, they would limp back to St. Louis, admitting failure; for with the supplies they had they could not possibly face the prospect of two more years in the field.

Meanwhile, they would cache much of their heavier equipment. This they would have done whichever turning they took.

They had learned the trick from the Indians. They dug circles in the sod, about twenty inches across, and this sod they removed, placing it to one side. Then they dug holes between six and seven feet deep, and lined these with buffalo hide and based them with a rickle of sticks calculated to draw off unwanted moisture. The supplies to be stored were placed in these holes, which were then covered with sticks and sod, the loose earth itself being dumped into the river. In a few days a stranger without a map, even though he might be looking for such a cache, never would have detected it.

Among other things they put their blacksmithy equipment into one of these holes, first holding a final inspection of all arms. They also risked a good part of their precious gunpowder, in lead caddies that kept it dry but were heavy.

Then Clark with one small party went south, and Lewis with another went north. They would find out for themselves.

Clark went forty miles up the south fork, which he decided, definitely, was the Missouri. Lewis went sixty miles up the north fork before deciding, at last, that it was not the Missouri but another, unnamed river. On the way back he made up his mind that he would name this flat and muddy stream after an admired friend and cousin back home, Maria Wood.[31]

Because he had gone farther, both by boat and on foot, Lewis was two days later in the search than was Clark, and when he rejoined Clark at the fork he found his fellow captain, worried, forming a search party. It was not often that these two were separated for more than a few hours at a time. Nobody had ever heard them quarrel.

They took the south turning. The men all shook their heads, but they were soldiers and they went where they were told.

The men were wrong, the captains right. They were still on the Missouri, which stretched toward the mountains. They could see those mountains now, the Rockies, gleaming in the distance, their tops all white. Just the other side of them, they hoped, would be the headwaters of the River of the West, whether that was the Columbia or another. They pushed on.

Game was plentiful, and easy to bring down. These animals never had seen or heard a gun, and some of them were so tame they could be approached and clubbed to death, saving powder.

The way led to the north of the black, drear Bad Lands, which would not have been good country for game.[32] They were near enough, sometimes, so that the explorers could sniff the sulphur from still-burning fires deep in the earth.

The river now was only 100 to 150 yards across, a trickle to what it had been below. It twisted more capriciously than ever, and was jampacked with islands. There were some cottonwoods and some willows and many shrubs, but almost no honest-to-goodness trees. The banks were rocky and steep, veritable mountains in themselves; and high up, and at a considerable distance, they saw large numbers of big-horned ibex, which scampered on their tiny hooves from crag to crag with perfect aplomb. They managed to bag one of these, and they kept its skull for the President.

They saw much Indian sign—a lost moccasin, a lodge, some leather tepees, the remains of camp fires—but no Indians. This troubled them. They knew that they had been seen. Some of the camp fires appeared to be only a few days old, and from time to time smoke wavered against the western sky, which meant that savages were signaling to one another, no doubt announcing the approach of the Corps of Discovery, which they, never having seen white men, would assume to be a war party from the east. Sacajawea was able to tell them that the moccasin was not Shoshonean, and they supposed that it had been dropped by a marauding Blackfoot. Sacajawea, however, could not read the smoke signals. After all, she had been no more than a girl when she was taken away from her people.

They had been told by the Mandans, who knew them only as far-off enemies, that the Shoshone Indians had many horses, beasts they had presumably obtained, in the first place, from the Spaniards to the south. The Corps very much wanted to buy some of those horses. Without horses, as they saw it, they would never get themselves and their supplies over those mountains.

It was the fear of the captains that if they came suddenly upon the Shoshones it might be in the form of an ambush. The savages, having seen them from afar, would be prepared to fight. This of course the explorers did not want. A battle, howsoever small, inevitably would ruin their plans. It was for this reason that they arranged a new formation, one of the captains, now Lewis, now Clark, then Lewis again, alone or with two or three men going on foot ahead of the main body. They hoped in this way to make contact with the Shoshones quietly and be given a chance to persuade them of the newcomers' pacific intentions.

The main party itself, the men in the canoes, would raise every flag the Corps commanded. No Indians would go to war flying flags.

This was the reason that Captain Lewis was all by himself when he came upon the Falls of the Missouri.

10

The Lone Horseman

He MUST HAVE HEARD THEM, the thunder of them, hours in advance, as he must too have seen the great arched iridescent cloud of spray that hung like gossamer above them. Even so, the appearance of the falls themselves took the breath out of him. It was "the grandest sight I ever beheld."

There were in fact five waterfalls, each tremendous, and they were joined by a series of rough, noisy rapids. This would mean a long portage. Lewis sat down to marvel and to wait for the others.

When Clark came, and despite the fact that his feet hurt him, he insisted upon surveying the entire territory for the purpose of mapping out a "road" or route around the falls. This he did. It was sixteen miles long, and very steep, very rocky. Much work would have to be done on it before any of the supplies could be moved.

They cached some more materials here. The men, being American soldiers, had accumulated many souvenirs at the Mandan villages, and they were urged to leave these behind. Even so, some kind of wagon must be built.

They found, nearby, a cottonwood tree that measured twenty-two inches across the base, a giant, "perhaps, the only one of the same size within 20 miles," and out of this they made wheels. These were not very good wheels, nor did the sawed-apart mast of the white pirogue make a pair of very good axletrees. The resulting vehicle, indeed, was almost unbelievably cumbersome, and kept breaking down; but it was the best that they had. Both of their horses had long since become lost, and the Mandans had been unable to sell them any, so that at first they had to push this ungainly contrivance. Then somebody had the idea of mounting the mast of the red pirogue in the middle of the wagon and spreading a sail upon it. They still had to push, but not so hard. When the wind was right, they reckoned, that sail was equal to four extra men.

All the time, night and day, there sounded in their ears the thunder of the falls, but they had no time to sit and enjoy the view.

It was backbreaking, it was heartbreaking work. The miserable cottonwood split and cracked. The weather had never been worse—torrential rains and hail—nor had the mosquitoes and the buffalo gnats. Prickly pears, particularly thick there, cut the feet.

The weatherman did not even relax his malice for the national holiday. July 4 the men were given the day off and, though there was nothing special in the way of food, the last of the whiskey was poured out: thereafter the Corps of Discovery was to be utterly liquorless. Some of the men took to dancing, to the tune of Cruzatte's faithful fiddle, but a cloudburst sent them scampering for their tents.

To make matters worse, this was where Captain Lewis decided to launch his collapsible iron boat. He decreed that it too should be carried over that terrible sixteen-mile portage and launched in the river above the falls. The pirogues, deemed too large for this trip, they would hide at the foot of the falls. The *Experiment* would take the place of both of them, and the six small dugout canoes would take care of the rest.

The idea had been to assemble the *Experiment* and then sheath it with birchbark. There was no birch anywhere in this wild land, so Lewis elected to try elk skin. Extra hunters were sent out, and twenty-eight such skins were used, besides four buffalo hides. Unfortunately they shrank when they were put into the water, and this stretched the holes through which the tying threads had been passed, so that the craft leaked badly.

Lewis, it would seem, had been over-ingenious. It had been a part of his plan to provide against leaks by caulking the *Experiment*, once it had been assembled, with tar. The tar he would have made from the bark of coniferous trees. But—there were no coniferous trees along the upper-upper Missouri, any more than there were any birches. Desperate, they tried a mixture of powdered charcoal and beeswax, together with some buffalo tallow. Then they put her into the water, where to Lewis's delight she floated. It was a different story the next morning. The caulking had caked and peeled off, and the boat was on the bottom.

They had already spent almost a month at the Falls of the Missouri, and if they did not get over those mountains to the west soon the passes would be filled with snow. There was nothing for it but to let the *Experiment* lie there—at least it would not be seen by the Indians, if there *were* any Indians in this Godforsaken country—and hope to pick it up on the way back.

The going was hard, the stream very narrow, the current fast. Oars no longer could be used, or a sail. Poling, or, in the shallows, pulling, were the only means of propulsion.

Game was not as plentiful as it had been below the

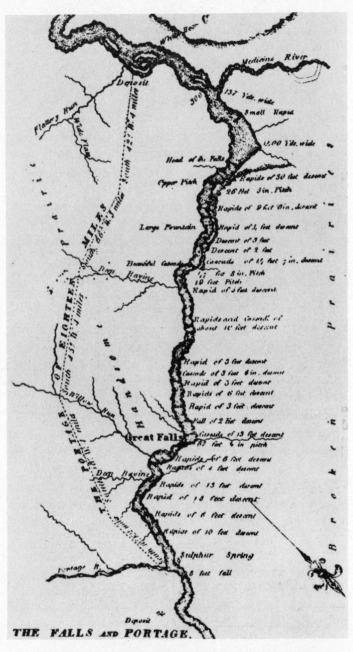

White Bear C.

Medicine River

Deposit

300 137 Yds. wide

Small Rapid

5,00 Yds. wide

Flattery Run Wide Plain

Head of the Falls

Upper Pitch

Rapids of 30 feet descent

26 feet 5 in. Pitch

Rapids of 9 feet 6 in. descent

Large Fountain

Rapid of 6 feet descent

Descent of 3 feet

Descent of 3 feet

Beautiful Cascade

Cascade of 14 feet 7 in. descent

47 feet 8 in. Pitch

19 feet Pitch

Rapid of 3 feet descent

Dog Ravine

Rapids and cascade of about 14 feet descent

Rapid of 3 feet descent

Cascade of 3 feet 6 in. descent

Rapid of 3 feet descent

Rapids of 6 feet descent

Rapid of 3 feet descent

Fall of 2 feet descent

Great Falls

Cascade of 13 feet descent

87 feet 6 in pitch

Rapids of 6 feet descent

Rapids of 4 feet descent

Dog Ravine

Rapids of 13 feet descent

Rapid of 18 feet descent

Rapids of 6 feet descent

Rapids of 10 feet descent

Sulphur Spring

8 feet fall

Portage R.

Deposit

Prairie

MILES

THE PORTAGE OF EIGHTEEN

Willow Run

Sulphur

Pranir

Broken

THE FALLS AND PORTAGE.

MAP BY WILLIAM CLARK OF THE AREA SURROUNDING
THE GREAT FALLS OF THE MISSOURI

E. S. PAXSON'S PAINTING OF THE LEWIS AND CLARK PARTY AT THE THREE FORKS

Falls. The hunters would be gone for long periods of time. Yet the explorers were eating nothing *but* game, for they wished to save their grains for the higher lands, and of course they had no vegetables. Now and then they would get a few wild berries, but most of their food they shot. At this time, just short of the Rockies, the thirty-two men and one woman would eat every twenty-four hours four deer, or one elk and one deer, or one buffalo.

Shannon got lost again, and was not found for three days.

Shields was badly bruised when a loaded dugout scraped over him as he lay on the bottom. Had the river been a couple of inches less deep he would infallibly have been crushed to death.

Charbonneau, Sacajawea, and Captain Clark, not to mention the papoose, Baptiste, narrowly escaped a similar fate when they were almost trapped in a narrow chasm during a cloudburst that in seconds filled the gorge with rocks and with mud.

The Corps proceeded through an eerie tunnel-like pass where the rock walls rose sheer on either side, cutting off the sight of everything but a slit of sky. They called this the Gate of the Mountains.

The Bird-Woman was sick, and so, much of the time, was Meriwether Lewis.

They were going largely south, a little west. There were mountains on both sides, but the real ones, the big ones, were on the right, to the west.

They came to the Three Forks. That was July 25.

They would hide a canoe from time to time, as their impedimenta lessened, but with the stream getting so narrow and so shallow, and its banks so rocky and steep, poling the remaining canoes, or, more often, pulling them, was an increasingly onerous task. Clark, who had a bad ankle just then, was left in charge of this, while Lewis, a geyser of impatience, all one fret, pushed ahead in search of redskins. Lewis took with him Privates McNeal and Shields and the hunter-interpreter Drewer.

August 11—it was a Sunday—they came upon an Indian road. This they followed eagerly—until it faded from sight. Anxious to pick it up again, Lewis ordered Drewer to comb the ground to his right, Shields that to his left, while Mc-Neal, who carried high an American flag, trudged along behind him.

They were heading in the general direction of a pass in the mountains ahead, a pass Sacajawea had told them led to the homes of her people.[33]

The men were given strict instructions not to shoot, no matter what the provocation. Lewis was convinced that the Indians were near at hand, perhaps watching them at that very moment, and one shot might frighten them away. If Shields or Drewer wanted to call the captain's attention to anything, he should raise his hat at the end of his rifle; but he *must not* shoot.

It was thus that they were deployed when they met the Indian.

He was alone, and he was riding slowly across the plain, right toward them. He was about two miles away. Meriwether Lewis, a Virginian after all, immediately perceived, with a spyglass, that the horse was an "eligant" one. Lewis was more interested in the horse, indeed, than in the rider, of whom at first he could only see that he was dressed differently from any redskin yet encountered, and that he carried a bow and a quiverful of arrows, and that he rode bareback. He did not seem to have seen the white men.

Lewis put his rifle on the ground, and proceeded at his usual pace. At a distance of about a mile the Indian, obviously having seen them, came to a halt.

The Indian did not seem to be alarmed. He was a statue.

Lewis unfastened a blanket from his pack, and grasping two corners of this he waved it three times above his head, finishing each flourish by spreading the blanket on the ground. This, he had been told, was the traditional sign language for "friend"; it indicated hospitality.

The Indian did not stir.

Lewis walked on, without his blanket, without his rifle or his spyglass, which he had left on the ground. He noticed with alarm that Drewer had emerged from the cover on his right, Shields from that on his left, and though they must have seen the Indian they marched straight ahead, as they had been ordered to do. They were both a little in advance of their commanding officer, who had lost some time by his blanket-waving act. In a few minutes one or both of them would be alongside the lone horseman, and in a minute after that they or he would be *behind* him. No Indian was going to stand for such a state of affairs.

The distance was too great for a shouted command to reach them. Lewis signaled for them to stop. Drewer did so, but Shields kept on.

Lewis fished out some beads and other trinkets, brought along for this very purpose. He waved these above his head as he walked.

The Indian did not move.

He was only about a hundred paces away now.

Lewis, whose face and hands were about the color of those of the Indian, thanks to constant exposure to the weather, rolled up a sleeve of his shirt and pointed to his white forearm.

"*Tabba bone,*" he cried. "*Tabba bone!*"

He had previously asked Sacajawea for the Shoshone word or phrase for "white man," and this was what she had told him. In fact, the Shoshones had no word for white man. Why should they? "Tabba bone" meant, in their language, "stranger" or "outsider," and this the newcomers obviously were, having no need to announce it.[34]

There was scarcely a trace of uniform among them, and no military emblems, and Lewis certainly would have left his sword back in one of the canoes. Their boots had long since been worn out and discarded, and they were shod in made-on-the-trail moccasins. Small wonder that the Indian was puzzled.

"Tabba bone!"

It was too late. Shields had advanced to a point where he could be thought to be at least partly behind the Indian. The Indian wheeled his horse and galloped away.

Meriwether Lewis was a highly emotional man, and he berated his assistants, especially Shields, who protested that he had not seen the signal to stop.

McNeal, in a moment of exuberance, or perhaps hysteria, bestrode the silly little stream they had been following, and with a foot on each bank spread his arms and in a loud voice thanked God that he could step clear across the once-mighty Missouri;[35] but Captain Lewis had no time for such histrionics, and he ordered an immediate advance along the track left by the redskin's elegant mount. This led them right into the high gap in the mountains, and there, since it was getting dark, and since he was certain that the Indians were watching them from many high places nearby, Lewis ordered a fire built. Around this fire he placed his brightest trinkets —looking-glasses, hole-punchers, and the like.

A sudden heavy fall of rain spoiled this plan when it put out the fire. The same shower washed away the tracks left by the Indian's horse.

They spent the night in that pass, right smack *on* the

A Charles Bodmer painting of the Rocky Mountains, as they might have appeared to the time the expedition passed through

CHARLES M. RUSSELL'S MURAL OF LEWIS AND CLARK MEETING THE FLATHEADS

Great Divide, and in the morning they continued west, going sharply downhill now.

They came to the beginning of a westward-running river, their first, clear and cold, and Meriwether Lewis drank of it, happy, as he declared, at last to know the Columbia.[36]

They had got over the Hump.

11

Getting to Know Them

Gᴇᴛᴛɪɴɢ ᴛᴏ ᴋɴᴏᴡ the mountain tribesmen was to prove a much less difficult feat than the encounter with the lone horseman would seem to forecast. The first thing next morning, Meriwether Lewis and his companions started along the same dim trail, gifts or flags in their hands, their eyes busy, ears cocked; and soon they saw, on a nearby hillside, an Indian man, a squaw, and several dogs. They approached these cautiously, waving baubles, having left their guns behind, but the pair did not await their arrival and nipped into the cover of the nearest bushes. The explorers could not even make friends with any of the dogs, though they tried. The captain had hoped to fasten toys around the necks of these animals, to show peaceful intent; but they were too shy.

A little later, however, the men espied three females, one young, another much younger, no more than a girl, and the third an old crone. The young squaw scampered out of sight, but the other two, at the approach of the strangers, bowed their heads obediently as though to acknowledge that they were prepared for death. Instead, the newcomers gave them beads and painted their cheeks red, which delighted them. The other squaw, the one who had run away —but not, it would seem, far away—now came back; and they painted *her* cheeks too.

They did this not in order to introduce these savages to the glories of Caucasian cosmetics but rather because they had been told that a face painted red among the Indians in this part of the world was universally taken to be an expression of peaceful intent. Whatever the reason, the women were pleased.

Now there came, at a gallop, a party of about sixty braves, all armed with bows and arrows and with tomahawks, except that three of them had rusty muskets. These reined to a halt, puzzled by the glad faces of the squaws and by the appearance of the men whom they had supposed to be Minnetarees on the warpath.

The squaws held up their beads, giggling, and pointed to their painted cheeks.

Drewer, who was the best at this, broke into sign language, striving to convey the impression that all was well and that no harm was meant.

After a while the Indians dismounted.

The chief, a tall, haggard personage named Ca-me-ah-wait, or something like that, suddenly threw his left arm around Lewis's neck and hugged him and pressed his cheek against his. The others all followed suit. The captain somehow survived this affecting if singularly greasy treatment. He got out a redstone pipe, and he got out a carrot of tobacco, and he proposed, by signs, that they have a smoke. In a matter of minutes they were all seated on the ground, their legs crossed before them, while the pipe was being passed from one to the other.

The Shoshones—and they were surely Shoshones—took off their moccasins. This was something new to the visitors. These tribesmen, as they were soon to learn, were not much different from those of the upper Missouri. They did have a Jewsharpy sort of instrument they called a thrapple, but for the most part their idea of music was similar to that found in the Mandan villages—that is, rudimentary. They were fond of all sorts of beads, feathers, ribbons, anything bright, and they liked to have their garments flamboyantly fringed. Their dances were no more than a lugubrious, nonpatterned shuffle. Their councils were characterized by pipe-smoking, a great deal of grunting, and hours-long oratory. However, the taking off of the moccasins was a gesture unfamiliar to the members of the Corps of Discovery. It meant, they soon learned, that the bare-footed one was saying in this way that he wished to walk through life without any footwear if he did not with all his heart welcome the current guest as a friend. This was a comforting thought.

There was another though lesser difference in ceremonial procedure. As Lewis and his companions were to learn, when they had rejoined Captain Clark and the rest of the party and had gone to the nearby Shoshonean village for a larger, full-dress council in a real lodge, the redstone pipe, always used among the Arikaras, the Mandans, the Minnetarees, and the Sioux, did not exist here high in the mountains. It had been replaced by a stumpy thing, barely two and a half inches long, of some dense transparent green stone that was strange to the visitors. The tobacco, however, was the same —very weak, very bad.

It was of course not customary to admit squaws to such serious sessions, but Sacajawea was present at this one since she was indispensable as an interpreter. Her work in this capacity, however, was hampered by the fact that she had

SACAJAWEA RETURNING TO HER PEOPLE

recognized one of the chiefs as her own brother, which caused her to weep for joy, not giving her full attention to the task at hand. The brother, for his part, did not seem much interested.

The Shoshones were a poor people. Starvation always stood at their backs. Once they had roamed the great plains and had practiced the bison economy, but the Pawnees from the south, the Sioux from the east, the Blackfeet from the north, each of them much more numerous than the Shoshones, had chased them back into the mountains where there was very little game of any kind. They would sally forth in strong hunting parties in the spring and sometimes in the fall, all the while watchful for any sign of their enemies, and quickly kill as many of the buffalo as they could, taking back to the mountains the hides and as much of the meat for jerking as they were able to carry They lived on that meat, more or less, for the rest of the year. They might bring down an occasional bird, but there were not many of those. They could seldom get near enough to an elk or a deer to kill it with their bows and arrows, and the few muskets they had no longer worked. Their staple food was roots. Of necessity they had learned to find and to dig up all sorts of edible roots other Indians might never have known about. It was unexciting fare and not readily available, but it was the best that they had. They were like animals in their incessant search for food.

The Shoshones had never even heard of maize, and when the Corps of Discovery men gave them the few ears they still had left they were delighted.

The captains, like the other keepers of journals in this band, seldom wrote any comments on the weaponry of the Indian tribes encountered on the way. Presumably this was because there was nothing new about it. The white man was so far ahead of the red man in the invention and development of lethal devices that it was useless to study the ancient, clumsy bows and spears of any warrior race, even one as far west as this one. They did, though, make a note of the *poggamoggan,* which caught their eyes.

It was a Shoshonean shillelagh, twenty-two inches of wood covered with dressed leather, "about the size of a whip handle." Fastened to one end by means of leather thongs was a stone that weighed about two pounds. At the other end was a loop for a man's wrist. Swung in combat, whether from horseback or by a man on foot—it was not thrown, being too heavy—the poggamoggan could be a formidable weapon.

The Shoshones *did* have horses. These, or at least their ancestors, undoubtedly had come from the Spaniards to the south. They were good horses, but not well trained. They were half wild, and, if let out to pasture, had to be hobbled. The Shoshones protested that they were short of horses just at that time, and could spare but a few, yet they did not ask much for them. The first three went for trade goods to the value of about twenty dollars, the next for "an old checkered shirt, a pair of old leggings, and a knife." Eventually more than thirty changed hands.

The Shoshones also had some mules, and they valued these much higher than the horses, possibly because they could not breed them. One mule, by their calculations, was worth two horses, or three, or even four horses. The explorers were not interested in mules, which is odd when the beast's surefootedness in hilly places is considered, and their course, after all, would lead over mountains. They probably were not familiar with the mule, never an ingratiating animal; but every man jack of them knew how to handle horses.

Having no metal of their own, the Shoshones were keen to get metal goods. The women, especially, were fascinated by the small steel punches or awls, with which they could

THOMAS JEFFERSON,

PRESIDENT

OF THE UNITED STATES OF AMERICA.

From the powers vested in us ———— by the above authority : To all who shall see these presents, Greeting:

KNOW YE, that from the special confidence reposed by us in the sincere and unalterable attachment of *Mar charka Metacta* a *flancis ———* of the *Sosus* NATION to the UNITED STATES ; as also from the abundant proofs given by him of his amicable disposition to cultivate peace, harmony, and good neighbourhood with the said States, and the citizens of the same ; we do by the authority vested in us, require and charge, all citizens of the United States, all Indian Nations, in treaty with the same, and all other persons whomsoever, to *————* acknowledge, and treat the said *War charfa ———* *his Nation* in the most friendly manner, declaring him to be the friend and ally of the said States : the government of which will at all times be extended to *their* protection, so long as *they* do acknowledge the authority of the same.

Having signed with our hands and affixed our seals this *Thirteenth* day of *August* 180*four*

M. Lewis Capt.
1st U.S. Regt.

W. Clark Capt.
59th Artillery
& Co.

PRESIDENT JEFFERSON EMPOWERED LEWIS AND CLARK
TO ISSUE INDIAN COMMISSIONS SUCH AS THIS TO IMPORTANT CHIEFS.

make holes in leather, holes through which laces and thongs could be passed. The Mandans had liked these too, and the explorers did not have many of them left. They were running short of colored beads as well, and of mirrors.

They liked the Shoshones, an honest people, a straight-forward people, and comparatively clean. They noted that the squaws were better treated than squaws had been else-where, and as a result were stronger and lived longer. On a minor food-hunting expedition Private Whitehouse noted: "One of our Indian women was taken sick a little back of this and halted a fiew minutes on the road and had hir child and went on without Detaining us." [37]

Nevertheless, they had to think of the weather. They were over the hump, true, but just *barely* over it; and the real Rockies lay ahead. They reminded one another of this.

Winter came early in those parts. Only a few days after their first contact with the Shoshones—it was August 19, a Monday—they awoke in the morning to find all the grass whitened by frost. On September 4 the ground was covered with snow.

Lewis's exuberance at finding a westward-flowing stream soon faded. Their hosts disillusioned them. True, the Lemhi fell into the Kooskooskee,[38] the Kooskooskee into the Snake, and the Snake into the great Columbia itself; but the Lemhi and much of the upper Kooskooskee were impassable, the Indians said emphatically. Lewis did not credit this. He sent out a party to examine the Lemhi, and these men re-turned with shaking heads: it was all too true, they said. Other plans had to be made.

They must go right over the mountains, and they must go immediately. They persuaded a Shoshone with an un-pronounceable name—they called him Old Toby—to go with them as a guide. Old Toby took along his four sons, making that many more mouths to fill, but three of them deserted early in the trek, presumably to make their way back to the Shoshonean villages.

Now there came a terrible time. The trail was steep, the footing sharp, so that their moccasins and the feet inside them were slashed in many places. Their tarpaulins froze. The wind was cruel, all poniards. Snow flew: on the 16th there were six to eight inches of it. The horses got skittish and tried to run away.

Hunger was what hurt the most. They even finished Captain Lewis's portable soup. They had been carrying twenty pounds of bear oil, and they drank this in search of sustenance. The hunters went out ahead, usually with Captain Clark, but they got precious little in that barren waste —a few pheasants,[39] a small gray species of squirrel, a blue bird "of the vulture kind about the size of a turtledove or jay," and, blessedly, one wolf. They ate the candles. Soon they began to eat the horses.

There was a great deal of diarrhea and dysentery. The men were weak, and their stomachs shrieked with emptiness.

It was necessary to allow the horses to graze from time to time, in order to keep up *their* strength, and on these occasions they tended to slip away. One day, two of the men were told off to try to round up a couple of mounts that had escaped in this manner. They were two of the stoutest men, but they staggered like drunkards and could hardly keep their feet, so acute was their pain. They did not recover the horses, and soon, barely able to move, they turned back. It was easy to pick up the trail of the main party, but they began to fear that they would not be able to overtake that party. When they came upon the remains of a camping place by the side of a small stream—the men had named it

Hungry Creek—they were about ready to quit, to drop to the earth and quietly die. But there was a surprise in store for them. It was at this camp—and the ashes of the fire were still warm—that the men had slaughtered and eaten the first horse. Only its bones and hooves and head remained. The head had been rolled to one side as inedible. The two starving men fell upon it, and finished it raw—ears, cheeks, eyes, lips. This enabled them to make one last try, and they caught up with the others.

It was an army of scarecrows—*sick* scarecrows—that at last, on September 19, tottered into a Nez Percé village on the banks of the Kooskooskee.

It was perhaps their appearance that saved their lives. The Nez Percés (pronounced "purses") had never before seen white men. They were a much larger tribe than their friends and neighbors the Shoshones, and they could easily have wiped out these sickly newcomers. They held a hasty council and decided not to. After all, who wants to slay a skeleton? Instead, pitying, they offered their hospitality.

Meriwether Lewis was in a state of total collapse—men on either side had been holding him in his saddle for the last few miles—and he was unable to smoke the pipe and to make his accustomed speech about the Great White Father in Washington. William Clark did this for him. Clark also demonstrated the use of the Harrison air gun; and York, his servant, as popular as ever, though he was getting mighty tired of this act, once again submitted to many wet-finger rubs. Most of the men, exhausted, could take no part in the ceremony.

Captain Lewis was to be out of things for a whole week, but by the end of three days a few of the men had got to their feet and saluted Captain Clark, asking for orders. These were set to work making canoes. The Corps of Discovery had

had its fill of land travel. Hereafter it would be all on water.

They chose pine, probably ponderosa, for their canoes, five in number, and for the first time they did not *hack* these out with axes and adzes but *burned* them out, as the Indians had advised.

They branded their remaining horses and turned them over to several well-connected braves, to whom they gave hatchets and a few trinkets. They would pick up the horses on the way back, they hoped.

They buried their saddles, together with some lead and several cannisters of gunpowder.

Monday, October 7, 1805, they set forth.

It was not easy. The stream was stippled with rapids. There were portages beyond count, and several times canoes were upset or were stove in, necessitating a delay while the trade goods were dried, the damage repaired.

The men still were weak, many of them prostrate, unable to help with the poling and the paddling. The banks were too steep to permit of hunting parties, and they subsisted now chiefly on fish, which they caught as they went along, and roots, which they bought from the Indians.

These Indians were not at all like the upland Nez Percés and Shoshones. They were shifty and shameless, unabashed thieves, the women as well as the men, and they would bargain with a wiliness all but Oriental. Moreover, they were beset with fleas. The captains as often as possible avoided entrance into any of their tents. The lodges where the councils were held were bad enough. No matter how hard they tried, the explorers could not shake off these pests, which swarmed everywhere, indoors and out.

The eastern side of the mountains they must often have thought of as the Land of the Grizzly. The western side assuredly was the Land of the Flea.

The Kooskooskee emptied into the Snake, another treacherous, rude river, and in time the Snake emptied into the fabled Columbia, itself no millstream.

They were still shooting rapids, when they were not carrying the canoes around portages.

One thing was notable about these flea-bitten redskins. For the most part, they did not gawp upon the members of the Corps of Discovery as though they were visitors from another planet. Since these Indians lived fairly near the sea, most or even all of them had at least heard of white men, and many must actually have seen them in the form of fur traders off Yankee or English or Russian ships.

The trip down the Columbia at times must have seemed interminable, yet, as they neared the mouth of the Columbia, there were little touches to gladden the heart. In one village they came upon an Indian who was proudly wearing a pea jacket. In another they overheard one Indian in anger call another a "son of a pitch," and *then* they knew for sure that at last they were getting close to the edge of civilization.

It was a day of pouring rain, November 7, when there was an unexpected and even dramatic lull. The rain ceased for a little while, the fog rolled back, and there, ahead of them, gleaming a dirty gray, lay the Pacific Ocean. Then the fog rolled in again.

CHAPTER

12

Gray Days at Fort Clatsop

Iт RAINED. It always rained, it seemed—ardently, ve-
hemently, with malice. It had been raining for three days
before they even spotted the Pacific from afar, and it was to
rain for almost a week after they got to the mouth of the
Columbia, blowing so, and piling up such high seas, that they
could do almost nothing about examining their surroundings,
but crouched perforce under the overhang of some rocks,
doubtless saying, with Habakkuk, "Oh Lord, how long?"

They pulled their canoes far up on the beach, and in-
verted them, to keep them out of the reach of the hissing,
grabbing waves.

The Spaniards, who discovered it, had at first called the
Pacific Ocean the Southern Sea, no doubt because Balboa
was facing south from the Isthmus of Panama when first he
looked upon it, and that name to a considerable extent had
persisted, so that most of the members of the Lewis and
Clark expedition probably thought of it as the Southern Sea,
even while they cursed it. Certainly it was anything but
pacific, as they met it. It was dark, angry.

They had accomplished their mission. They had established beyond all doubt that the Northwest Passage did not exist, that despite all rumors and bright stories there was no practicable continuous water route between the Atlantic and the Pacific.[40] This should have made them happy; but as they crouched under those rocks all they could do was pray that it would some day stop raining long enough for them to dry out some of their gear, hunt for game, and even set up tents.

Everything was rotting. Woolen cloths, even strips of canvas, would come apart in their hands.

When at last they were able to move around they scouted both banks of the river for several miles back from the sea, and then they held a council, a novelty for them, in which everybody had a vote. They decided to build their fort on the southern bank. The hunters said that game was more plentiful there, and Sacajawea said that on the south bank she could dig up more wappato, a potatolike root of which she was fond. They settled not upon the majestic Columbia itself but upon the west bank of a tributary a few miles from the Columbia's mouth, a stream the Indians called the Netul.[41]

Here they built Fort Clatsop. It consisted of two parallel buildings made of fir and white cedar, of which there was plenty nearby, each building about fifty feet long and rectangular, the whole being enclosed in an eight-foot palisade with a gate and sentry box at the south end. The west building, for the men, was divided into three rooms, each sixteen feet square and with a fireplace in the middle but no chimney: they were very smoky. The east building had two officers' rooms, each with a fireplace *and* chimney, and a separate storehouse. The parade ground was 48 by 20 feet. The sentry box was manned night and day, and the gate was kept locked all night every night. As at Fort Mandan, the rule was that Indians could be inside the grounds in the daytime but never after sundown.

The place was named for the Indians who lived nearby, a rather scruffy tribe like all those in the Columbia River Valley. The Clatsops gave no trouble, though they had to be watched because of their thievish habits. Their chief, a personage named Comowool, was given a pair of satin breeches, and he was the white man's friend for life. Medals too were handed out, as was the custom.

The Clatsops were no better but neither were they any worse than the other small, mean, dirty Indian tribes of that part of the world. They would steal anything they could get their hands on. They went back on bargains. They were eaten up by fleas. Syphilis and gonorrhea were endemic among them, though in a mild form. Like so many other primitive peoples, not to mention Europeans until recently, they had many superstitions about the menstruation of their women, who in these periods were kept locked in special houses far away from all the others.[42] They had no sense of female chastity. A button off your coat would get you a squaw for the night, though, as among the Mandans, the Minnetarees, and the Arikaras, that button would be paid not to the squaw herself but to her husband, or, if she was unmarried, to her father.

The Chinooks, the Cathlamahs, Killamucks, Lucktons, Cookoose, Shalalahs, Luckasos, and the Hannakalais, Chilts, Killaxthokle, Youitts, Lickawis, Youkones, Necketos, Ulseahs, Shiastuckles, Clamoitomish, Potoashees, the Quinnechants —there was not much to choose among them. Like the mountain redskins, they fancied blue beads and, to a lesser extent, white beads, but they had no overwhelming fondness for red beads, though they did love red feathers and bits of red

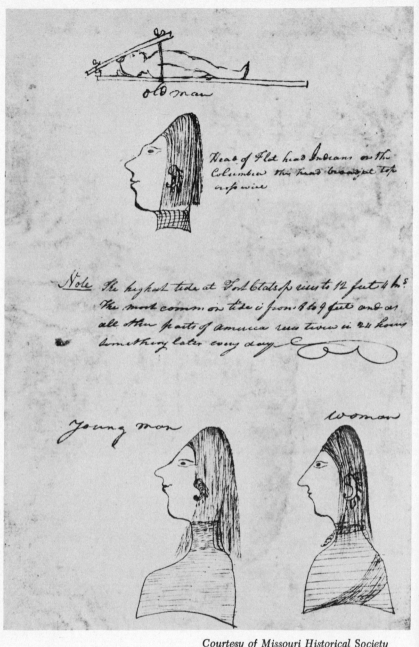

Courtesy of Missouri Historical Society

THIS PAGE FROM WILLIAM CLARK'S JOURNAL ILLUSTRATES
HOW THE CHINOOK INDIANS FLATTENED THE HEADS OF THEIR
CHILDREN, AND THEN HOW ADULTS LOOKED.

egt which the string pass to fasten the round pieces which pass crosswise the Canoe to strengthen & left her.

This form of a canoe we did not meet with untile we reached tide water or below the great Rapids.

from thence down it is common to all the nations but more particularly the Kil a mox and others of the Coast. these are the largest Canoes, I measured one at the Kilamox village SSW of us which was   feet   feet wide and   feet d   this a

CLARK'S DRAWING OF A COLUMBIA RIVER CANOE
ACCOMPANIES THIS JOURNAL ENTRY.

ribbon. The explorers never could understand this. By the time they reached the west coast they were virtually out of blue beads.

These Indians *were* different from most others in that they sometimes bathed, or at least the men did, or some of the men. The explorers often noticed the sweat-sheds they had built. These were small, and were placed over piles of rocks which were heated and then doused with water, the resulting steam going up into the shed, occupied by one man at a time. Afterward this man customarily would dive into a stream of cold water. The explorers believed that this was a therapeutic rather than a lavatory process, but they never were sure whether it was meant to soothe the syphilis from which these men suffered, or the flea bites, or both. They were not, themselves, tempted to try it.

123

One thing could be said in favor of the Columbia River Indians: they made beautiful canoes, elaborately carved at bow and stern. Some of them even had crude totem poles, for this was the southern edge of the totem culture.

They all had different languages or at least different dialects, and in most cases they could understand one another only by means of signs. All these dialects and languages the captains studied, making "vocabularies" of each.

In most respects the redskins, without any pride, freely acknowledged their own inferiority. They whined; they cringed, pleading for trinkets. In two matters, however, they actually looked down upon the white man. The canoes he made were clumsy, ugly things. And he ate dogs. To the Clatsops and their unsavory cousins there was always something queer about a man who ate dogs.

The members of the Corps of Discovery had developed this habit up-country, among the Shoshones and the Nez Percés, where hunger was a condition, starvation always near at hand. Those Indians certainly were not fussy about their food. They would eat horses, entrails and all. Yet it never seemed to occur to them to eat the dogs with which their villages were filled. They used these dogs as beasts of burden when they moved from place to place, as small horses. They did not hunt with them, and never taught them to retrieve. And certainly they did not seem to regard them as pets, for they did not treat them with any affection and did not feed them, but allowed them to forage for themselves. Nor did they make any objection when the white men offered to buy them, though it was patent what the white men meant to do. Rather, the Indians were amused, and mildly contemptuous. The Dog-eaters, they called the white men. This had been true back in the mountains, and it was even more true among the miserable tribes of the lower Columbia, non-dog-eaters all.

The white men did not mind. They had taken to the consumption of dogs originally as a measure of desperation. The very idea, they had found at first, was repulsive. But soon they had formed a fondness for this kind of food. Once the early squeamishness had passed they realized that they preferred dog to elk, which they never had liked much, and even to venison and the lower river fish. The captains separately recorded that the times when the party existed on a strictly canine diet were exactly the times when the men were the most healthy.

At the fort time limped. The men were put to work making new and stronger canoes, using the fir and cedar that abounded in the region. Hunting parties were always out, and parties were sent up or down the coast in the hope —vain, as it proved—of seeing or hearing of the arrival of a ship. Still another party spent many long weary hours boiling the salt out of seawater, so that they could preserve their extra meat. And there was always guard duty.

A sperm whale 105 feet long was washed ashore only a few miles away, and they went to see it. The Indians already had stripped away the meat and blubber, and there was nothing left but the skeleton, which was too large to send to the President. They did, however, take careful measurements of that skeleton.

They brought down the biggest bird any of them ever had seen, the biggest indeed in America, a California condor (*Gymnogyps californianus*). It was nine and a half feet from wing tip to wing tip, three feet ten and a half inches from point of bill to tip of tail. The tail itself was fourteen and a half inches long, the head and beak six and a half inches. The captains both recorded it as a vulture. They had been much troubled by vultures of late, and often their game was half eaten before they could bring it in.[43]

Christmas Day the captains passed out the last of the

tobacco—to the men, not to the Indians, who had their own tobacco and were welcome to it. Such men as did not smoke were given silk handkerchiefs. It was not a joyous occasion.

New Year's Day they danced a bit, but they did not put much heart into it. The Indians, as always, loved to watch them dance. They would come from miles around to witness the spectacle. It was now 1806.

Most of the time, because of the drenching rains, they could do little or nothing out of doors. It was never as cold as it had been the previous winter at Fort Mandan, where at one sunup their thermometers had registered 45 degrees below zero; but it was cold enough. It was wet, raw. The rain sometimes would change to snow, and then it would change back again.

For two months there were only four days without rain.

From November 4, when they first got into the lower Columbia River country, to March 25, two days after they had started back up the river, had started east, there were only twelve days without rain, and six of those were not really clear.

Regretting that there was never a ship off that coast, so that they might have sent their records and some of their men back by way of the sea, they packed their supplies, gathered their gear, and wrote and signed a batch of statements about the expedition, each including a list of its members. These statements were passed out among certain chiefs with instructions to give them to any fur traders who might appear off the coast. In this way, it was hoped that, if the expedition should be wiped out on the way back, at least

Courtesy of Missouri Historical Society

THIS DRAWING OF A SALMON-TROUT SHOWS HOW WILLIAM CLARK
FREQUENTLY ILLUSTRATED PAGES OF HIS DIARY.

This is a likeness of it; it was 2 feet 8 inches long, and weighed ten pounds the eye is moderately large; the pupil black with a small admixture of yellow and the iris of a silvery white with a small admixture of yellow and a little ... tirbed near its border with a yellowish brown.

the position of the fins may be seen from the drawing, they are small in perportion to the fish. the fins are boney but not pointed except the tail and back which are a little so, the ... fin and ventral ones, ten rays; those of the ... and the small fins the tail above has ... but is a tough flexable ... covered with smooth ... perportion to its ... Salmon. the ... head on each ... subulate teeth the ... before ... fish ... with

fins
prime back
contains each
gills twelve,
placed near
no long rays,
...able substance
skin. it is thicker in
wedth than the
tongue is thick and firm
border with small
in a single series.
of the mouth are as
described. neither this
nor the Salmon. are cought
the hook, nor as I know on
what they feed. —— —
now began to run. &c,

some record of it would survive. They were taking with them the journals themselves and all their scientific material.

They gave the fort to old Chief Comowool of the satin pants, and shoved off in their rickety little canoes. It was Sunday, March 23, and raining.

13

"The Dirtiest and Stinkingest Place"

THEY WERE NOT YET to get rid of the fleas—not for a long while. When actually in the canoes and engaged in paddling upstream they could stay tolerably clean, but there were rapids to be gone around and there was food to be collected, and horses. These tasks involved contact with the Columbia River Indians, who were more surly than ever, often insolent, always thievish.

Because they were anxious to get over the Rockies in time to make St. Louis that year, rather than be hung up for another winter in the Mandan villages while the Missouri was choked with ice, they had pushed off before the annual running of the salmon. They hoped that the salmon would somehow catch up to them.

They had jerked or salted as much meat as they conveniently could—most of it deer and elk—but this had to be saved for the mountain crossing, which would take at least a week, and which, as they knew from experience, would be conducted in a foodless land. Meanwhile, and as they went upstream, they would live largely on fresh dogs and pounded roots, both of which would be purchased from the river tribes.

Lewis was ill during much of this time, and it was up to William Clark to handle the land business, to haggle with the redskins. It was he who had to endure the stench, the insults. "The village of these people is the dirtiest and stinkingest place I ever saw in any shape whatever," he was to write in his journal March 24, "and the inhabitants partake of the carrestick [characteristics] of the village." [44]

Treating with these peevish brutes was the more difficult because the Corps of Discovery now had almost no trade goods left—no blue beads at all, no white beads, only a few red ones, and no mirrors, no gimlets, not many fishhooks. Yet they desperately needed dogs, and because they could not be sure that any of the horses would be left when they returned to the land of the Nez Percés they believed that they needed horses.

Clark solved the problem by setting himself up as a physician. He took part of the medicine chest with him, and he suffered the disabled and the sickly to come unto him, which they did in large numbers. His fee was a dog, or, in really serious cases, a horse. If the petitioning patient had no such animal Captain Clark simply refused to treat. He had been lucky; but, after all, he was not a real doctor and he hadn't taken the Hippocratic oath.

Meanwhile Meriwether Lewis was struggling with the canoes.

The farther they got from the Pacific the less offensive were the redskins, and the men actually liked the Wallawallas, who were, indeed, some kind of cousins to the Nez Percés.

The Wallawallas had a prisoner, a Shoshone, and the explorers questioned him concerning the land that lay ahead and the habits on the plains of the predatory Pawnees and Blackfeet. This interview took a long time, though they did not learn much. It was a cumbersome process. A question would be put to the half-breed Drewer, in English. He would pass it along, in French, to Charbonneau, who in turn, using the Minnetaree language, would ask it of his wife, Sacajawea, and *she* at last would render it into Shoshone for the benefit of the prisoner. The answer of course would come back in reverse.

They had certainly set forth too early, in their eagerness to get over the Rockies as soon as ever the snows would permit. Among the Nez Percés, on the banks of the upper Kooskooskee, they had to spend almost a month, from May 14, exactly two years from the day they had started up the Missouri, to June 10.

May 9 they did get back most of their horses, though about half of the saddles and "some" of the gunpowder were gone. The Nez Percé left in charge of these, one Twisted Hair, complained that the white men had not made their cache cleverly enough. Because of the condition of the mounts they did get back—many had saddle sores—they felt sure that Twisted Hair had rented them out to friends; but they said nothing about this. After all, what with the horses William Clark had purchased along the Columbia they had more than forty when at last they threw themselves at the Bitter Roots.

They did not make it the first time. They returned, chagrined, to the Nez Percé villages, where they offered three strong young braves two rifles—not muskets—to go along as guides. They had to add to this gunpowder and lead before the braves consented. Fortunately their lead, like their powder, still was in good supply, and they had a heap of it cached ahead, by the Great Falls of the Missouri.

They of course left their canoes behind. They did not just abandon them. They sold them—or tried to sell them. When the Columbia River Indians—Clahclellahs, Quinults, Calasthortes, whatever they were—refused to pay even a few dogs, the Corps of Discovery men chopped the boats up for firewood.

The second time, they did make it over the mountains. It was touch-and-go for a while, but they never suffered the way they had suffered when they traveled west on this same trail the previous fall.

A Peace medal given to the Nez Percé chief, Twisted Hair, by the expedition

Then they did a curious thing. They split their little force. Almost two-thirds of it, including Charbonneau and Sacajawea and the baby, went south with Captain Clark, to hook around Pompey's Pillar—it was Clark who gave it that name [45]—and reach the Yellowstone River, where they would build canoes and float down to the Missouri. Meanwhile, Captain Lewis, with nine men and the Indians, went north of the Missouri's headwaters with the idea of exploring Maria's River more carefully. It was Lewis who would unearth the supplies cached near the Great Falls, and later he would rejoin Clark somewhere near the place where the Yellowstone empties into the Missouri, and from there they would proceed downstream to the Mandan villages, after which they could face the Teton Sioux in force.

It was their belief that they took little risk in this split, for they were unlikely to meet any hostile Indians between the Rockies and the Mandan villages. In this they were mistaken. Clark had no more than minor misadventures as he explored the whole long, lovely valley of the Yellowstone, but Lewis, on the upper Maria's, ran spang into a war party of Indians.

They were Minnetarees, but Minnetarees of the Plains, quite different from the Upper Missouri Minnetarees whom the explorers had known so well.

The white men were outnumbered by more than two to one—Lewis had only three men with him, Drewer and the Fields brothers, the others, under Sergeant Gass, having been ordered to await them at the mouth of the Maria's—but they had a marked superiority in weapons.

Lewis was cool. He put aside his rifle and took out his redstone pipe, and he proposed that they have a smoke. The Minnetarees agreed. Seated, they passed the pipe around, as each side boasted, in sign language, that it was only an outflung scouting party and that it had a large force to fall back upon nearby. Such talk was customary in the circumstances, but here, oddly enough, each side *believed* it.

It is wrong to attack a man with whom you have smoked the pipe of peace, but the thought of those rifles—those long, beautiful Kentucky rifles—was too much for the Minnetarees, who, in the dark of the night, long after they had all wrapped themselves in their blankets and lain down together around the same fire, tried to steal them. A drowsy sentinel, Joseph Fields, awoke shouting; and in the fracas that ensued two of the redskins were killed, one of them by Lewis himself. They fled to the north, while the white men, equally alarmed, fled to the south.

The cache at the Great Falls proved to be only a half-success. Water had got to the botanical specimens, ruining them. Water too had damaged the reserve medical supplies, but much of this damage could be and promptly was rectified. The powder and ball and the canoes were in perfect condition.

No member of the Corps of Discovery had been so much as scratched in the course of the shoot-up on Maria's River, but Meriwether Lewis himself was to be a casualty—at the hands of one of his own men.

The explorers of the upper Maria's had united with Sergeant Gass's command at the mouth of that river, and hastened on down the Missouri. They had failed to find the Clark party at the mouth of the Yellowstone, but they did find there a note saying that mosquitoes had made the place unbearable, causing the men to drop downriver in search of a more comfortable spot.

Lewis and Cruzatte went hunting. Lewis got a deer and together they wounded another, which plunged into the underbrush. They went after it.

Now, Pierre Cruzatte was a spirited violinist and he was also a first-class boatman, which is the reason he had been signed on; but he was blind in one eye and extremely near-sighted in the other, not at all a man you would pick for a hunting companion. Captain Lewis was clad in buckskin, the last bit of his military uniform long since having been given to greedy chiefs, and when, peering out of some bushes, he heard a shot nearby and felt a terrible burning at the place where ordinarily he sat down, he assumed that Cruzatte had made a mistake, taking *him* for the wounded deer. "Damn you, you have shot me!" he cried; but there was no answer. The pain was intense, and he knew that he was losing a lot of blood back there, so he called again to the Frenchman; and again there was no answer. Alarmed, he wondered in a flash whether those Indians from the upper Maria's had led a scalp-hunting party against them. Where *was* Cruzatte? Was he already dead, stabbed from behind? Lewis, despite the pain, and despite the fact that his breeches were filling with blood, somehow made his way back to the canoes, where he collapsed.

A party went forth, soon to return with an abashed but intact Pierre Cruzatte, who swore that he had not heard his commanding officer call. They also brought the second deer, which they had cornered and killed.

The ball had passed through both of Captain Lewis's buttocks, fortunately without hitting a bone or an artery. Even after he himself had patched it as best he could, the wound stung him; and it was a long time before he could sit down or sleep on his back.

No charges were brought against Cruzatte, though neither did anybody again ask him to go hunting.

William Clark and the ailing Meriwether Lewis met once more, without fanfare, on the banks of the Great Muddy a little distance above the Mandan villages, August 12, 1806. They had been separated since July 3.

The Mandans made a big to-do about them, urging them to stay for a long while, but after some pipe smoking and canoe patching they pushed on south, along the home stretch.

They left behind them one of the privates, John Colter. He did not desert. He had met up with a couple of American trappers in the Mandan villages, and he had agreed to go pelt-hunting with them up the valley of the Yellowstone if his commanding officer would let him off. Lewis let him off, giving him the two and a half years' pay that was his due. First, however, Lewis questioned the others, to make sure that they did not entertain any such ideas, for he didn't want this to develop into a fever. The others assured him that they did not. All they wanted was to get home.

They left behind, too, Charbonneau and Sacajawea and the papoose, Jean Baptiste, Clark's "Little Pomp." Captain Clark offered to take the baby with him to St. Louis and see that he was educated, but the parents thought that he was still too young.

Thus they were only twenty-nine in number when they set off on a south-by-southeasterly course down the Big Muddy.

The Teton Sioux gave them no real trouble. There was some name-calling and there was some fist-shaking, but no shots were fired. The river is wide at this point, and the Corps of Discovery prudently stayed in the middle, ignoring the savages along the shore.

They waxed perhaps a whit cocky, they pressed their luck a little, when, near home, they tried to travel at night. They rounded a sharp curve and were sucked into "a parsel of sawyers," which tossed them hither and yon and almost

By the last Mails.

MARYLAND. BALTIMORE, OCT. 29, 1806.

A LETTER from *St. Louis* (*Upper Louisiana*), dated *Sept.* 23, 1806, announces the arrival of Captains LEWIS and CLARK, from their expedition into the interior.—They went to the *Pacific Ocean*; have brought some of the natives and curiosities of the countries through which they passed, and only lost one man. They left the *Pacific Ocean* 23d March, 1806, where they arrived in November, 1805;—and where some American vessels had been just before.—They state the Indians to be as numerous on the *Columbia* river, which empties into the *Pacific*, as the whites in any part of the U. S. They brought a family of the Mandan indians with them. The winter was very mild on the *Pacific*.—They have kept an ample journal of their tour; which will be published, and must afford much intelligence.

ONE OF THE FIRST NEWSPAPER REPORTS
OF THE RETURN OF THE EXPEDITION

swamped the whole expedition then and there. When they had straightened things out they pitched camp, giving up night travel. They had only learned again what they already knew: that you can't trust that river.

At the trading post of La Charette they could call themselves back in civilization again. There for the first time in fourteen months they got whiskey, two gallons of it. They had to pay eight dollars for this. *Eight dollars.* The captains fumed, but they paid.

Tuesday, September 23, 1806, they paddled proudly into the proud little town of St. Louis, ending a long but successful trip.

CHAPTER

14

He Did the Deed

IT IS REMARKABLE that though they traversed or at least touched upon places that were to become ten different states—Missouri, Nebraska, Kansas, Iowa, South Dakota, North Dakota, Montana, Idaho, Washington, and Oregon—besides the Illinois from whence they had set forth—none of these was named by them or after them.

The captains were cautious nomenclators. They did not give way to high spirits at the sign of an as-yet-nameless hill or stream. They left behind them no Git-Up-and-Gits, or Poker Flats, or Delirium Tremens, or Shirttail Gulches, as did those who were to come later, notably the Forty-Niners. They felt posterity breathing down the back of their necks, and they were dignified, though never pompous, when it came to making another entry on a map.

Just at first the travelers had found that most of the really memorable landmarks already had been named by Frenchmen, the first whites in those parts. They seldom changed these names, though often they did render them into English. Thus, the river that the French had called the

Roche Jaune (which itself was probably a translation of its Minnetaree name, Mitsiadazi) they wrote down as the Yellowstone; the Ile de Vaches became Cow Island; the Loup became the Wolf River; an island upon the beach of which the French had found many smooth stones, and which they had named Le Boulet, the Lewis-Clark party translated into the Cannonball. Soon, however, this expedient failed. The French had not gone as far as the Rockies.

Whenever the first Spanish explorers of the New World came upon an island, a headland, a stream or a peak that had never before been gazed upon by white men, they had two recourses. They could name it after the saint on whose day it was discovered, or they could name it after the sailor or the member of the land party who first had spotted it—or after somebody nominated by him. The Americans, being Protestant, did not have a handy hagiology, and they were reluctant to honor their own kind, perhaps because they feared to seem to play favorites. There was, to be sure, and still is, a Clark's Creek. There was a Lewis River, but this soon became the Shoshone, and a little later the Snake.

They did not succumb to the current fad of the classical, and specified no Romes or Carthages or Athenses. Sometimes the reason for the name was obvious, like Lone Pine Hill. The streamlet they came upon on July 4 quite naturally was dubbed Independence Creek. Ever mindful of their patrons, they named a Jefferson River, which is still so called, and a Gallatin, a Madison, a Smith, and a Dearborn, after members of the cabinet. The three tributaries to the Jefferson they rather self-consciously named the Philosophy, the Wisdom, and the Philanthropy, which in time have become, respectively, still another Willow Creek, the Big Hole River, and the Passamari, which in Shoshone means "stinking water."

Sometimes, especially with the humbler, more familiar animals, they used the name that they had brought from

home and always had known—the katydid, for instance, was
a chittydiddle—but, when strangers were uncovered, new
names had to be devised. Our explorers described twenty-
two new kinds of fish, six new birds, five new reptiles, four
new amphibians. Yet of the names they gave to these creatures none have survived, while only two—the Lewis wood-
pecker and Clark's nutcracker or crow—were named *after*
them by more learned latecomers to the field.

The reason is that the captains Clark and Lewis did
not know Latin, and the scientific community has decreed
that no plant or animal can really exist until it has been clas-
sified by one of their own kind and in a language only they
can understand. Lewis, true, had been the President's secretary; but, with a man so energetic and so prodigiously learned
as Thomas Jefferson, little secretaryship was needed. Lewis,
in fact, had no more than a typical frontier education, which
meant almost no education at all in the formal sense of the
word. Clark, one of the world's worst spellers, had rather
less than that. Therefore they could not name a new animal
or plant and expect the name to stick. Such immortality as
this amounts to was reserved for more cloistered naturalists.

Yet our captains did not go unhonored. For a whole
year and a half after they vanished into the wilderness no
word of them had emerged, so that when at last they burst
upon the frontier capital of St. Louis there was a deep-
throated shout of welcome, followed by a swirl of congratu-
latory dinners and balls, first in St. Louis itself, then in
Louisville, and later, at least for Lewis, in Washington.

While they were wintering in Fort Clatsop, Clark's
commission as second lieutenant in the army had automatically been raised to one of first lieutenant. He now resigned
this. However, both men were immediately raised to brig-
adier generalships, Clark of the Louisiana militia, Lewis of
the regulars. Congress with commendable alacrity voted to

double the army pay of everybody who had taken part in
the expedition, and to grant to each private 320 acres of
public land, which most of them sold right away, and to
Lewis 1,600 acres, to Clark 1,000 acres. Lewis promptly ob-
jected. Though official Washington persisted in regarding
Lewis as the real commander with Clark as a mere adjutant,
Lewis himself always avowed that their ranks were equal.
Congress, which was ready to grant almost anything just at
that time, agreed to this, raising Clark's grant to 1,600 acres.

After the Louisiana Purchase the vast new territory had
been divided into two parts. The southern part, to be known
as the Territory of Orleans, its capital New Orleans, extended
from the Gulf of Mexico to the thirty-third parallel of latitude,[46] while the northern part, with St. Louis as its capital,
was all the rest, and was to be called the Territory of Louisiana.

Meriwether Lewis was appointed governor of the Territory of Louisiana, and William Clark was appointed principal agent for Indian affairs there.

Clark did very well. He fitted the post, and adorned it.
Chief Red-Head always had liked the Indians, and within
the bounds of his ability he understood them and was always
ready to hear their side of the story and to stand up for
them. The job was no sinecure. Despite the peace treaty
between the Mandans and the Arikaras that he and his partner had so laboriously negotiated during that memorable
winter on the upper Missouri, these two tribes were at war
with each other again. The Sioux too were kicking over the
traces. The incoming American traders, not always morally
admirable, were jostling the old Frenchmen, who resented
it, and antagonizing, too, the redskins. The United States
and Great Britain seemed to be on the verge of war, and
British traders out of Canada were increasingly pushy. But
the principal agent for Indian affairs was a happy man, a

well-adjusted man, and he took everything in his stride, never losing his head, never raising his voice.

He had eschewed the giddy delights of lion-hunting Washington when he returned from the wilds, making instead for Virginia and "Judy" Hancock, the girl after whom he had named a river. He had wooed and won her, and now, in St. Louis, they were engaged in raising a fine healthy family. They named their first son Meriwether Lewis Clark.

The principal agent was putting on weight, but his blue

JULIA HANCOCK

eyes remained genial and his door always was open to his friends, white and red, who were legion.

It was not thus with Governor Lewis. He was out of his element. He was expected to be at once a politician and a skilled civil executive, and he was by nature neither. His nervous temperament, his fitful disposition—even in the field he had been subject to bouts of blackest despair—did not belong in a place where placidity was called for. He tried to be fair, adjudicating among the land speculators, but perhaps he tried too hard; and he made many enemies. He speculated himself, not too wisely. He was short of funds and obliged to borrow. Washington was asking for an explanation of some of his gubernatorial expenditures; and though he could explain them readily enough, this would have been hard to do at such a distance.

Many men in politics were jealous of him because he so obviously owed his position to his friendship with President Jefferson, but Jefferson would not be in the White House much longer, and what then, when Governor Lewis came up for reappointment? His second-in-command, Frederick Bates, the secretary of the territory—a position equivalent to a lieutenant governorship—positively hated Meriwether Lewis and wanted his job. Bates was a pompous polysyllabic fellow but no fool, nor was he overburdened with scruples.

Early in the autumn of 1809, then, troubled, Lewis decided to make a trip to Washington in order to meet the new President, James Madison, and to show all his papers and prove his innocence of any possible charges of wrongdoing. (There were no such charges, but at the time he had some reason to think that there might be.)

There were three ways of going from St. Louis to Washington. One was by barge poled up the Ohio to Pittsburgh, the rest of the way by land. Another was by way of Natchez

and Nashville, overland. The third, and the one Lewis decided upon, was all water—down the Mississippi, into the
Gulf, and on around.

At Chickasaw Bluffs,[47] at Fort Pickering commanded
by his friend Captain Gilbert C. Russell, he changed his
plans. All the clack had it that war with Great Britain was a
mere matter of weeks away, perhaps only days. One of the
first things that the British Navy would do was cap the mouth
of the Mississippi. Probably they already had made plans
for this project. And if General Lewis fell into their hands,
a legitimate prize of war, he might never get to Washington
with his papers, and might never clear his name. He decided
to go by land instead, over the Natchez Trace.

It had a dark name. Little more than a series of Indian
footpaths, not wide enough for a wagon, it extended in a
generally northeast-southwest direction between the Mississippi and the Cumberland. That was wild country. Most of
it was owned and more or less occupied by the Choctaw and
Chickasaw, but these, who held it by treaty, were not the
troublemakers. White desperadoes with their long knives
were what gave the Trace its reputation. Keelboat men who
had floated down the Ohio and the Mississippi to New Orleans, where they had sold both cargo and boat, habitually
returned to Kentucky, to Ohio, to Pennsylvania, overland
by way of the Natchez Trace. These men had money with
them, cash. When they traveled in groups, as customarily
they did, they were all right; but let one of them go it alone,
or lag behind his fellows, and the chances were good that he
would never be seen again. It was easy to hide a corpse in
that wilderness.

The governor of the Territory of Louisiana arrived at
Fort Pickering on September 15, and he remained there for
two weeks. He was a sick man, though just what was the

matter with him we probably never will know. He was feverish, and some of the time his talk was incomprehensible. There were those who would say, afterward, that he had in this time twice tried to take his own life, but there are no details of this, and, indeed, no verification. There were also to be those who would say that he was drunk, or at least recovering from a bad bout of drunkenness; but this too is unlikely, for Meriwether Lewis never had been much of a man with a bottle. Whatever the reason, he was still pale and shaken September 29 when he left the fort, and Captain Russell, who had just lent him one hundred dollars, was worried about him.

Lewis had purchased or hired a saddle horse and two pack horses, and to these latter beasts were fastened some of his personal baggage and all the red leather-bound books of the journals he and Clark had so conscientiously indited. He hoped to get them published.

He had a young Creole servant named Pernia, and he was accompanied also by Major James Neelly, the Chickasaw agent for those parts, and Neelly's small Negro servant or slave. Neelly had his own horse. The boys went on foot.

The Memphis road joined the Natchez Trace at a place called Big Town,[48] and they stayed there for two days, for what reason we do not know. The night of October 8–9, having crossed the Tennessee River, they slept at a place called Dogwood Mudhole, not far from the edge of the Indian territory, and that night the two packhorses somehow got away. Major Neelly in the morning said that he would go back and look for them, and Governor Lewis said that he would go on ahead, the boys trailing him. He instructed Neelly that he would stop at the first habitable white man's dwelling along the way.

In that desolate region such a house was not reached until almost sundown. There a woman, after shushing two small children, told the governor that she was Mrs. Robert Grinder and that her husband was helping with the harvest at a farm some twenty miles away. Yes, she could provide food and lodging.

He asked for whiskey, and she gave him some, but he drank only a little of it. He remarked on what a fine day it had been. When the boys came up he sent one of them out to get a cannister of gunpowder from a saddlebag, and with this he reloaded and reprimed the two pistols he carried. He also carried a dirk.

He ate very little supper, seemingly absorbed in thought, but afterward he lit his pipe and remarked upon what a lovely evening it was. When Mrs. Grinder started to prepare the bed for him he told her that he preferred to sleep on the floor, and he sent one of the boys out for a buffalo hide in his baggage. Perhaps he feared that the bed would be buggy.

Mrs. Grinder was to sleep in the adjoining kitchen with her children. But she did not sleep. She lay awake, listening to her guest as he strode back and forth talking to himself, "like a lawyer." She was frightened, this frontier woman. Even when two—or it could have been three—shots rang out, she did not get up to investigate. She heard the governor groan, and heard him beg for water, but she did not go to him and did not even open the kitchen door.

This was some time before dawn, possibly only a little after midnight. It would seem that the two servants, sleeping in the barn, did not hear those two or three shots, though the barn was only about two hundred feet from the house; or, if they heard them, they did nothing about it.

The governor got up, and staggered outside, seemingly in search of water. He went back inside, and fumbled with a water bucket, which was empty. He flopped down upon the bed he previously had scorned; and that was where they found him when at last, with the coming of daylight, they ventured in.

His forehead was torn half off, part of the brain exposed, and there was a bloody hole in his side. The pistols, empty, lay on the floor. He was still living—this was a good three hours after the shots had been fired—and in great pain. He groaned, and from time to time he would try to talk, but he said nothing that made sense. He lived for about three more hours.

A coroner's jury of six was assembled that same day. They examined the body and found a verdict of self-inflicted death. The body was then buried, right there.[49]

Mutterings about a murder were heard almost from the beginning, and they were to increase as the years wore away. A government post-dispatch rider who came along the Trace that very morning and had a good look at the body thought that Lewis had been shot from behind—in the case of the body wound—and that the wound in front was merely an exit wound. This man, one Smith, did not find any powder marks, nor did Major Neelly, who appeared soon afterward.[50] Neelly, a man with an excellent record both as an army officer and as an Indian agent, conducted a thorough search, but he never did find Lewis's watch, and he found no money, though Lewis certainly had had something like two hundred dollars on him.

Grinder, who appeared much later, was examined by a grand jury, but no charges were brought against him. He and his family soon afterward moved away, having bought another piece of land.

We will probably never know the truth.[51] It is certain that the men who knew Meriwether best, men like William Clark and Thomas Jefferson, never doubted that he had killed himself. But—they had not viewed the body. Whatever his health might have been, the man was certainly sober at the time; and his affairs, the event was to prove, were in good order: he was not desperate, not teetering anywhere near the edge of ruin. Also, two hundred dollars was a huge sum of money in that place and at that time.

CHAPTER

15

The Morocco-bound Books

A MAN COULD SPEND A LIFETIME studying the journals of the Lewis and Clark expedition. Men have. Scholars have specialized in certain aspects of the journals, in preparation for the composition of learned papers, while others have read them purely for pleasure, esteeming them the finest travel tales since Mungo Park, even perhaps since Marco Polo. Yet these same journals were to know trouble in finding their way into print; for publishers, who have never been noted for perspicacity, feared that they wouldn't pay.

There had been thirteen red morocco-bound volumes fastened to the backs of those misbehaving packhorses at Dogwood Mudhole—seven of them Lewis's, six Clark's. Major Neelly, after he had recaptured the beasts and after he had heard of General Lewis's death, dutifully saw to it that these were sent on to the War Department in Washington.

To a large extent these overlapped, each man having put down the events of the day. Lewis was the better educated, the more poetic, and from time to time he displayed

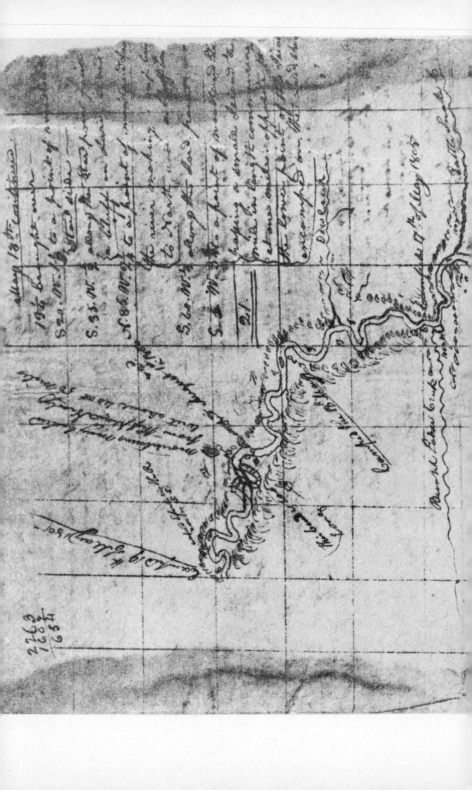

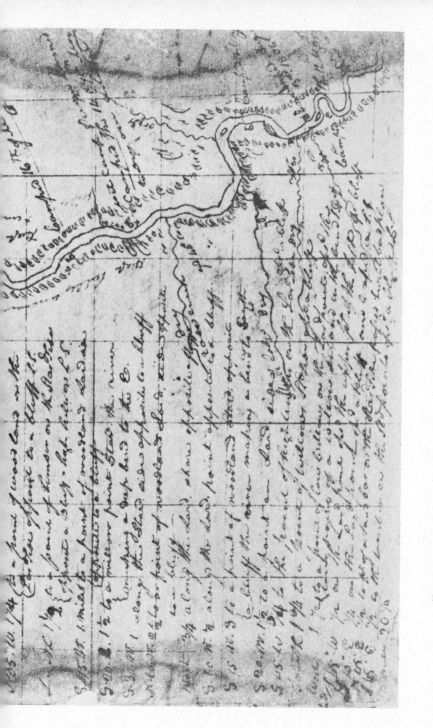

DETAILED MAP BY WILLIAM CLARK OF A SECTION OF THE MISSOURI RIVER

a quiet sardonic humor. The men must have compared notes before the actual in-camp penning, for Clark not infrequently followed Lewis's account word for word, though when he did write his own account he tended to be more laconic, more matter-of-fact than his partner.

Thomas Jefferson, in retirement at Monticello, pressed repeatedly for publication, which he took to be no more than a duty. He had assured both Clark and Lewis that though their report must be considered a public document they personally would be entitled to any profits that might result from its publication and sale. He predicted a good market for such a work.

Patrick Gass, the barrel-chested little Irishman who had been elected a sergeant to succeed Floyd, was a man of even less education than most of his fellows, but he too had conscientiously kept a diary, which he had no trouble getting into print after he had hired a literary hack, David McKeehan of Wellsburg, Virginia,[52] to pretty it up and to correct some of the grammar and much of the spelling. This book ran to some 83,000 words, and, coming out only a year after the return of the expedition from the wilds, it had an exceedingly good sale in this country and later in France and Great Britain. It was of course not official; neither was it inspired; but it was accurate and commendably thorough.

If Lewis had been the more "literary" officer, Clark had been the expedition's engineer. It was he who made the maps, and he, too, a gifted amateur, who drew the sketches of new forms of animal life. These he kept to himself, though with eventual publication in mind.

It had been their habit to jot down notes as they traveled, and when they were in camp for any length of time, and together, they would compare these notes and expand them. In St. Louis, when they had the time—for the first governor of the territory and its first agent for Indian affairs were very busy men—they would work these expanded notes over. The results of this last activity, all handwritten, in loose sheets, not bound, were contained in the thirteen leather-encased bundles Major Neelly had sent forward.

General Clark was offered the territorial governorship after the death of his friend, but he refused. Later, when it was offered to him again, he accepted; but for the present he was more concerned with getting those journals into print, if only as a memorial to his late friend Meriwether Lewis; and with this in mind he went East.

From the home of his father-in-law, Colonel George Hancock, near Fincastle, Virginia, he wrote to Nicholas Biddle of Philadelphia, asking that personage if he would consider editing the journals.

Biddle was only twenty-four, but already famous. At fifteen he had been graduated from Princeton. He had acted as secretary to the United States ambassador to France and in that capacity had straightened out the almost incredibly complicated spoliation claims in connection with the Louisiana Purchase. He had also been secretary to the ambassador to the Court of St. James's, and had traveled widely in Europe, before returning to Philadelphia to practice law.

Biddle was a youth of learning and much charm, and the demands upon his time were many. He wrote back to Clark regretting that "it will be out of my power to undertake what you had the politeness to offer," but exactly two weeks later, Philadelphia friends of Clark having talked earnestly with him in the meanwhile, he wrote again that "I will therefore very readily agree to do all that is in my power for the advancement of the work; and I think I can promise with some confidence that it shall be ready as soon as the publisher is prepared to print it." [53]

Biddle, at Clark's suggestion, paid a visit to Fincastle. Clark turned all the morocco-bound books over to him, in addition to lesser notes, maps, pictures, and the like. There were some 1,200,000 words of text alone. Clark also turned over to the distinguished Philadelphian Sergeant Ordway's diary, which he, Clark, had purchased from Ordway; and he made arrangements to have George Shannon, out of the army now, the youngest member of the expedition, available for questioning.

Thus equipped, the young lawyer went to work. Most of the volumes, as he finished with them, he deposited with the American Philosophical Society in Philadelphia,[54] though some of the lesser notes, together with the maps and the scientific matter, he sent back to General Clark, who by this time had returned to St. Louis to become the last governor of the Territory of Missouri, until recently called the Territory of Louisiana.

Though they had met for only a few hours, that day at Fincastle, Biddle and Clark worked well together at long distance. They had agreed to ask Dr. Benjamin Smith Barton of Philadelphia to edit and prepare for publication the scientific data collected by the expedition. He was a professor of medicine at the University of Pennsylvania and a vice-president of the Philosophical Society, and he was also one of those who had tutored young Captain Lewis in preparation for the great adventure. Barton gladly agreed, and the material was turned over to him. But he sickened and died suddenly, and thereafter for a long time this material did not see the light of day.

In spite of all his many interests, Nicholas Biddle labored mightily on the journals. He melded them. He trimmed them. He cut them into chapters. Usually he used the first person plural, "we" and "us," but when the two men had been apart he used the first person singular. He corrected the spelling and the grammar, and punctuated where punctuation was needed. He threw in classical allusions, as the literary conventions of the day required. All the while he was looking for a publisher. C. & A. Conrad of Philadelphia had agreed to do the publishing, but the long-expected War of 1812 at last arrived and times were hard on publishers, and C. & A. Conrad went into bankruptcy.

Biddle looked elsewhere—Thomas Bradford, Johnson & Warner, Bradford & Inskeep—but they were all leery of this masterpiece. At last he went back to Thomas Bradford, on Bradford's terms.

Biddle had lately been elected to the Pennsylvania legislature, and he believed that he could not finish the editorial job, so he hired a Philadelphia newspaperman, one Paul Allen, to prepare the manuscript for the printer. Allen was to be paid five hundred dollars by the publishers.

It was February 20, 1814—four and a half years after Lewis's death—before the journals were published, minus the scientific material and also minus the maps and sketches. There were two thousand copies printed, but somewhat over five hundred of these were somehow lost, whether by fire or by moldering unsold in some cellar. The work did not carry Nicholas Biddle's name as editor, and Allen got all the credit. At Allen's request, former President Jefferson had written a biographical sketch of Meriwether Lewis, and this was incorporated into the work as a sort of introduction, but even the author of the Declaration of Independence could not make a best seller out of the journals. After Allen had been paid, the profits were reckoned at $154.10. What happened to this money is not clear; but it is certain that neither William Clark nor the heirs of Meriwether Lewis ever saw a cent of it.

Born in wartime, a toddler at first, the journals soon came to be recognized as a travel classic, and there were many reprintings, though not until 1893 was there any attempt at a definitive edition. In that year Dr. Elliott Coues, who had been allowed access to the Philosophical Society papers as well as to many new documents recently dug up by Nicholas Biddle's descendants, brought out a four-volume work, the fourth volume of which was all maps.

Coues published much material that had not previously seen print, but he made it fancy, getting further than ever from the original homespun Lewis and Clark style. Also, new material was appearing all the time, from Biddle's heirs, from Dr. Barton's, and, almost casually, a gold mine from William Clark's. Mrs. Julia Clark Voorhis, granddaughter of the explorer, and her daughter, Miss Eleanor Glasgow Voorhis, both of New York, had, it now suddenly appeared, a vast amount of material that no living scholar ever had known to exist.

For these reasons, and also because a Louisiana Purchase centenary was coming up, the Philosophical Society engaged Reuben Gold Thwaites of the University of Wisconsin, an authority in the field, to make up a really definitive edition.

This he did, in 1904–1905, a hundred years after the expedition. It was in eight volumes. It stands today as *the* authority on the Lewis and Clark expedition.

Yet even it did not close the subject. Other bits and pieces continued to appear. John Ordway's journal, which had been missing for many years, and never had been published, was found among the Biddle papers, and it has been published by the State Historical Society of Wisconsin. The University of Illinois commissioned Donald Jackson to collect and edit all letters and other relevant papers connected with the Lewis and Clark expedition, extending from 1783 to 1854, and this he has done, a magnificent job. Most startling of all was the popping-up of William Clark's original field notes, a bombshell that exploded in the ranks of historians, librarians, antiquarians, and curators of museums.

These, sixty-seven scraps of paper, some only three inches long, were found in an old-fashioned rolltop desk in the attic of a Victorian house in St. Paul, Minnesota, in January, 1953. The house belonged to Mrs: Vaclav Vytlacil, wife of the artist, and the desk *had* belonged to her maternal grandfather, General John Henry Hammond, dead since 1890.

A Civil War hero, General Hammond had served for some years in the Bureau of Indian Affairs, and had known William Clark; but nobody, not even the general's relatives, suspected for a moment that he had such a treasure in his desk.

It had been assumed by those interested that Clark either used a slate for his field notes or pieces of paper that he later destroyed.

The notes are all in Clark's handwriting with now and then a few words in that of Meriwether Lewis. They are the more valuable because they pertain almost entirely to the winter spent in camp on Wood River before the active beginning of the expedition, and this is an aspect of the story not well known even to historians, for Clark and Lewis at that time had not yet started their journals.

Nobody could say how much those sixty-seven scraps of paper might be worth. Twenty thousand dollars was the smallest estimate.

There was a larger issue at stake, however. The federal government stepped in to lay claim to these papers on the ground that they were a part of the formal report of a United States Army officer who had been commanded by his commander-in-chief to carry out a certain mission. A copy of Jefferson's *Instructions* was produced in federal court in Minneapolis.

If the government won its case all sorts of valuable letters and other papers, in libraries and museums all over the country, might be subject to confiscation. Many institutions, not to mention many dealers, could be ruined by such an action. It was for this reason that the four-day trial, in itself not spectacular, was watched anxiously by the scholastic world.[55]

The government did not win its case. Yet it did not lose it *emphatically,* and it refrained from making an appeal. The matter thus remains open. The same thing might happen again.

The field notes themselves wound up, by gift, at Yale University, which published them in a handsome volume edited by Ernest Staples Osgood in 1964.

Is this the end of the story? Perhaps. But Sergeant Pryor's journal never has been found, nor have those of Privates Frazier and Shannon, nor any of the many Indian "vocabularies" the captains had so painfully compiled. Lewis and Clark, it would seem, die hard. We may yet be hearing more from them.

Notes

1. "The new ruler of France was not unused to failure. More than once he had suddenly given up his dearest plans and deserted his oldest companions when their success was hopeless. He had abandoned Paoli and Corsica with as little compunction as afterward he abandoned the army and the officers whom he led to Egypt. Obstinate in pursuing any object which led to his own advancement, he was quick to see the moment when pursuit became useless; and the difficulties that rose in his path toward colonial empire were quite as great as those which had driven him to abandon Corsica and Egypt." Adams, *History*, II, 14.

2. A century later, President Theodore Roosevelt was to take the same step in connection with the building of the Panama Canal. The public, impatient of delays, was yelling, "Make the dirt fly!" Two civilian engineers, J. F. ("Big Smoke") Stevens and John F. Wallace, had quit on very short notice, and the chief executive, furious, appointed George W. Goethals, head of the Corps of Engineers, United States Army, to the job. Goethals, being a colonel, *couldn't* quit.

161

3. That message, in full, is printed as Appendix A of this book.

4. The instructions are printed in full as Appendix B of this book.

5. ". . . such a craft as only an army officer would have designed." Bakeless, *Lewis and Clark,* p. 95.

6. There was no West Virginia then. It did not come into existence as a separate state until 1861.

7. *Letters,* 126–30.

8. It was near the present site of Paducah, Kentucky.

9. That is, it did *then.* It has since moved farther south.

10. The whooping crane, *Grus americana,* which still exists, if barely.

11. The place where they camped that night is now Kansas City.

12. The Forty-Niners, some years later, were to say of the Platte River that it was "too thick to drink, too thin to plow."

13. A wonderful bird is the pelican.
    His bill will hold more than his belican.
    He can take in his beak
    Enough food for a week,
    Though I'm damned if I see how the helican.

                                    DIXON LANIER MERRITT

14. This was not held on the site of the present Council Bluffs, seat of Pottawattamie County, Iowa, as popular report so long had it, but on the other side of the river, in what is now Nebraska, about twenty miles north of the present city of Omaha.

15. The bluff, though a "grave" is still pointed out to tourists, was soon washed away.

16. Both islands have long since been washed away.

17. They were to lose this peaceful disposition and to

become among the stubbornest opponents of the white man's westward push. At the same time they were to give up their abstemious habits, so that soon they would be as drunk as any other Indians on every possible occasion.

18. Louisville, Kentucky, today.

19. There is a local saying today to the effect that of all the variable things in creation the most uncertain are the action of a jury, the state of a woman's mind, and the condition of the Missouri River.

20. The entire tribe was to be wiped out, a few years later, not by the Sioux but by smallpox.

21. Approximately the site of the present Bismarck, North Dakota.

22. And with good reason. The Sioux, after having bawled out the Arikaras for having made peace with the Mandans, already, while the explorers were no more than reaching the Mandan villages, had in council formally declared war on them. Indian-fashion, they did not announce this declaration. That would wait until the attack, which would come in the spring. All this was designed against the white men only. The Sioux despised the Mandans. *Them* they could wipe out any Thursday afternoon, they believed.

23. At a later date such coats were to be made for this very purpose, and they were to be found very useful by a later generation of explorers in the South Seas.

24. This manner of dancing was to become very popular in the mining camps of the West in the middle of the century.

25. Sergeant Gass was, frankly, shocked. "It may be observed generally that chastity is not very highly esteemed by these people, and that the severe and loathsome effects of certain French principles are not uncommon among them," he was to confide to his diary, April 5, 1805. "The fact is, the women are generally considered an article of

traffic and indulgences are sold at a very moderate price. As a proof of this I will just mention that for an old to-bacco-box, one of our men was granted the honor of passing the night with the daughter of the head chief of the Mandan nation. An old bawd with her punks may also be found in some of the villages on the Missouri, as . . . in the large cities of polished nations." Coues, I, 252n. Biddle, the first editor of the Lewis-Clark journals, on coming to their description of the Mandan buffalo dance, a fertility rite, was constrained to put it into Latin.

26. Coues, I, 224.

27. *Letters*, pp. 231–34.

28. From the French *bois de vache*.

29. More twaddle has been emitted about Sacajawea than about any other Indian "princess," even the sainted Pocahontas. Poems have been written about her, and there is at least one biography. Statues have been reared to her, motels named after her. She has been hailed as the heroine *par excellence*, "a Shoshone Deirdre," in the words of Bernard De Voto (*The Course of Empire*, p. 478). She, they tell, saved the lives of the party by leading it through a hidden pass in the mountains, a pass remembered through all those years of captivity. This could be; but neither Clark nor Lewis, conscientious reporters, mentions it, nor do any of the other diarists. We do not know what Sacajawea looked like, though this has not prevented artists and sculptors from picturing her as a beauty. Sacajawea now and then might have dug up an edible root a white person would have missed, but she never saved the life of the expedition. On this particular occasion, however, her conduct was admirable, and she was warmly thanked.

30. She was to be married only a few years later to William Clark.

31. She too was to be married early—though not to

Captain Lewis. The stream is called Maria's River to this day, though customarily, now, without the possessive apostrophe.

32. The Bad Lands were to be described by a later visitor, General William H. Ashley, as looking "like Hell with the fires out."

33. The mountains were the Bitter Root Range, not yet named, and the pass is now called the Lemhi Pass after the river of that name. This was a part of the Great Divide located between Beaver Head County, Montana, and Lemhi County, Idaho, not far from Dillon, Montana.

34. An exact analogy would be the Hawaiian word "*haole*," originally "stranger," now "white man." There must be many others.

35. He was mistaken, according to modern geographers, who regard this stream as a mere tributary and locate the ultimate source of the Missouri River at the Three Forks. This is 2,464.4 river miles from the mouth at the Mississippi near St. Louis. This distance must have been much greater in the time of Lewis and Clark.

36. It was not the Columbia; but it was the Lemhi, which flows into the Columbia.

37. Thwaites VII, 142.

38. Today it is called the Clearwater.

39. This is what the captains called them in their journals—pheasants. In fact they must have been grouse. The two henlike birds are much the same, though the pheasant is a little heavier and has slightly longer legs. George Washington did have some pheasants sent to him from Europe and he tried to breed them at Mount Vernon, but they never "took." The present American pheasants, the ringnecks, were not brought to this country until 1860.

40. "The first major achievement was the demonstration that the last area of North America in which a commercially

practicable water route to the Pacific might exist did not contain one. In the long arc of history this ended the search for the Northwest Passage. And ending that chapter, it closed the volume which opened with the first voyage of Columbus." De Voto, *Journals,* xlix.

41. Today it is named the Lewis and Clark River. The site of the fort is near the present city of Astoria, Oregon.

42. Sir James G. Frazer has a whole chapter (LX) on this interesting subject. *The Golden Bough: A Study in Magic and Religion.* New York: The Macmillan Company, 1940.

43. This is still the largest American bird, measured by wingspread. It is also the rarest. There are only about forty of them left, and soon, it is feared, there will be none. Nobody alive today has ever seen one as far north as the Columbia River. The second rarest bird in America—and the tallest—is the whooping crane. There are about sixty of these left. Lewis and Clark saw hundreds of them overhead when they were in the lower Missouri.

44. Thwaites, IV, 200.

45. This landmark, a rock, almost round, its sides except for one steep slope virtually perpendicular, is about 200 feet high, 1,200 feet in circumference. Captain Clark named it after Sacajawea's papoose, Jean Baptiste, who, though he was nineteen months old now, had not yet been weaned. Clark used to call him, playfully, Pompey, a popular pet name for pickaninnies, or sometimes "my little Pomp." Clark carved his own name and the date on one side of this rock, near the base, where you can still read it.

46. The Arkansas-Louisiana state line of today.

47. Memphis, Tennessee, now.

48. Near the present Houston, Alabama.

49. A white granite shaft twenty feet high, four feet in diameter at the base and eighteen inches at the tip, marks

the spot, in Lewis County, Tennessee, about sixty-five miles southwest of Nashville. It was erected by the state of Tennessee.

50. The reader is reminded that the discovery of cordite was far in the future. The powder that Meriwether Lewis had in his pistols was black "firecracker" powder. The presence of unburned portions of this near a wound—if the shot had been fired from nearby—would have been much more conspicuous than that left by a modern cartridge.

51. "In the absence of direct and pertinent contemporary evidence to the contrary, of which not a scintilla exists, the verdict of suicide must stand." Phelps, *Tragic Death of Meriwether Lewis*, p. 317. "The evidence for murder is not very strong, and the stories from Fort Pickering strongly suggest suicide, but none of the evidence is really conclusive. It is impossible to make a positive statement, either way." Bakeless, *Lewis and Clark*, p. 423.

52. It is in *West* Virginia now.

53. Jackson, *Letters*, pp. 495–96.

54. Which still has them.

55. There is a lively account of this trial in *The New Yorker* magazine, in the issue of October 29, 1966.

Appendix A

Jefferson's Message to Congress

Confidential.

GENTLEMEN OF THE SENATE AND OF THE HOUSE OF REPRE-
SENTATIVES.

As the continuance of the Act for establishing trading
houses with the Indian tribes will be under the consideration
of the legislature at it's present session, I think it my duty
to communicate the views which have guided me in the
execution of that act; in order that you may decide on the
policy of continuing it, in the present or any other form, or
to discontinue it altogether if that shall, on the whole, seem
most for the public good.

The Indian tribes residing within the limits of the U.S.
have for a considerable time been growing more & more
uneasy at the constant diminution of the territory they oc-
cupy, altho' effected by their own voluntary sales: and the
policy has long been gaining strength with them of refusing
absolutely all further sale on any conditions, insomuch that,
at this time, it hazards their friendship, and excites dangerous jealousies & perturbations in their minds to make any

169

overture for the purchase of the smallest portions of their land. A very few tribes only are not yet obstinately in these dispositions. In order peaceably to counteract this policy of theirs, and to provide an extension of territory which the rapid increase of our numbers will call for, two measures are deemed expedient. First, to encourage them to abandon hunting, to apply to the raising [of] stock, to agriculture and domestic manufacture, and thereby prove to themselves that less land & labour will maintain them in this, better than their former mode of living. The extensive forests necessary in the hunting life, will then become useless, & they will see advantage in exchanging them for the means of improving their farms, & of increasing their domestic comforts. Secondly to multiply trading houses among them, & place within their reach those things which will contribute more to their domestic comfort than the possession of extensive, but uncultivated wilds. Experience & reflection will develope to them the wisdom of exchanging what they can spare & we want, for what we can spare and they want. In leading them thus to agriculture, to manufactures & civilization, in bringing together their & our settlements, & in preparing them ultimately to participate in the benefits of our government, I trust and believe we are acting for their greatest good. At these trading houses we have pursued the principles of the act of Congress, which directs that the commerce shall be carried on liberally, & requires only that the capital stock shall not be diminished. We consequently undersell private traders, foreign & domestic, drive them from the competition, & thus, with the good will of the Indians, rid ourselves of a description of men who are constantly endeavoring to excite in the Indian mind suspicions, fears & irritations toward us. A letter now inclosed shows the effect of our competition on the operations of the traders, while the Indians, percieving the advantage of purchasing from us, are soliciting generally our establishment of trading houses among them. In one quarter this is particularly interesting. The legislature, reflecting on the late occurrences on the Missisipi, must be sensible how desireable it is to possess a respectable breadth of country on that river, from our Southern limit to the Illinois at least; so that we may present as firm a front on that as on our Eastern border. We possess what is below the Yazoo, & can probably acquire a certain breadth from the Illinois & Wabash to the Ohio. But between the Ohio and Yazoo, the country all belongs to the Chickasaws, the most friendly tribe within our limits, but the most decided against the alienation of lands. The portion of their country most important to us is exactly that which they do not inhabit. Their settlements are not on the Missisipi, but in the interior country. They have lately shown a desire to become agricultural, and this leads to the desire of buying implements & comforts. In the strengthening and gratifying of these wants, I see the only prospect of planting on the Missisipi itself the means of it's own safety. Duty has required me to submit these views to the judgment of the legislature. But as their disclosure might embarrass & defeat their effect, they are committed to the special confidence of the two houses.

While the extension of the public commerce among the Indian tribes may deprive of that source of profit such of our citizens as are engaged in it, it might be worthy the attention of Congress, in their care of individual as well as of the general interest to point in another direction the enterprize of these citizens, as profitably for themselves, and more usefully for the public. The river Missouri, and Indians inhabiting it, are not as well known as is rendered desireable by their connection with the Missisipi, & consequently with us. It is however understood that the country on that river is inhabited by numerous tribes, who furnish great supplies of furs & peltry to the trade of another nation carried on in a high latitude, through an infinite number of portages and lakes, shut up by ice through a long season. The commerce on that line could bear no competition with that of the Missouri, traversing a moderate climate, offering according to the best accounts a continued navigation from it's source, and, possibly with a single portage, from the Western ocean, and finding to the Atlantic a choice of channels through the Illinois or Wabash, the Lakes and Hudson, through the Ohio and Susquehanna or Potomac or James rivers, and through the Tennessee and Savannah rivers. An intelligent officer with ten or twelve chosen men, fit for the enterprize and willing to undertake it, taken from our posts, where they may be spared without inconvenience, might explore the whole line, even to the Western ocean, have conferences with the natives on the subject of commercial intercourse, get admission among them for our traders as others are admitted, agree on convenient deposits for an interchange of articles, and return with the information acquired in the course of two summers. Their arms & accoutrements, some instruments of observation, & light & cheap presents for the Indians would be all the apparatus they could carry, and with an expectation of a soldier's portion of land on their return would constitute the whole expense. Their pay would be going on, whether here or there. While other civilized nations have encountered great expense to enlarge the boundaries of knowledge, by undertaking voyages of discovery, & for other literary purposes, in various parts and directions, our nation seems to owe to the same object, as well as to its own interest, to explore this, the only line of easy communication across the continent, and so directly traversing our own part of it. The interests of commerce place the principal object within the constitutional powers and care of Congress, and that it should incidentally advance the geographical knowledge of our own continent can not but be an additional gratification. The nation claiming the territory, regarding this as a literary pursuit which it is in the habit of permitting within its dominions, would not be disposed to view it with jealousy, even if the expiring state of it's interest there did not render it a matter of indifference. The appropriation of two thousand five hundred dollars 'for the purpose of extending the external commerce of the U.S.,' while understood and considered by the Executive as giving the legislative sanction, would cover the undertaking from notice, and prevent the obstructions which interested individuals might otherwise previously prepare in it's way.

TH: JEFFERSON
Jan. 18. 1803.

Appendix B

Instructions

To Meriwether Lewis, esquire, Captain of the 1st regiment of infantry of the United States of America: Your situation as Secretary of the President of the United States has made you acquainted with the objects of my confidential message of Jan. 18, 1803, to the legislature. You have seen the act they passed, which, tho' expressed in general terms, was meant to sanction those objects, and you are appointed to carry them into execution.

Instruments for ascertaining by celestial observations the geography of the country thro' which you will pass, have already been provided. light articles for barter, & presents among the Indians, arms for your attendants, say for from 10 to 12 men, boats, tents, & other travelling apparatus, with ammunition, medicine, surgical instruments & provisions you will have prepared with such aids as the Secretary at War can yield in his department; & from him also you will recieve authority to engage among our troops, by voluntary agreement, the number of attendants above mentioned, over whom you, as their commanding officer are invested with all the powers the laws give in such a case.

As your movements while within the limits of the U.S. will be better directed by occasional communications, adapted to circumstances as they arise, they will not be noticed here. what follows will respect your proceedings after your departure from the U.S.

Your mission has been communicated to the Ministers here from France, Spain & Great Britain, and through them to their governments: and such assurances given them as to it's objects as we trust will satisfy them. the country of Louisiana having been ceded by Spain to France, the passport you have from the Minister of France, the representative of the present sovereign of the country, will be a protection with all it's subjects: And that from the Minister of England will entitle you to the friendly aid of any traders of that allegiance with whom you may happen to meet.

The object of your mission is to explore the Missouri river, & such principal stream of it, as, by it's course & communication with the waters of the Pacific Ocean, may offer the most direct & practicable water communication across this continent, for the purposes of commerce.

Beginning at the mouth of the Missouri, you will take observations of latitude & longitude, at all remarkable points on the river, & especially at the mouths of rivers, at islands & other places & objects distinguished by such natural marks & characters of a durable kind, as that they may with certainty be recognized hereafter. The courses of the river between these points of observation may be supplied by the compass, the log-line & by time, corrected by the observations themselves. The variations of the compass too, in different places, should be noticed.

The interesting points of portage between the heads of

the Missouri & the water offering the best communication with the Pacific Ocean should also be fixed by observation, & the course of that water to the ocean, in the same manner as that of the Missouri.

Your observations are to be taken with great pains & accuracy, to be entered distinctly, & intelligibly for others as well as yourself, to comprehend all the elements necessary, with the aid of the usual tables, to fix the latitude and longitude of the places at which they were taken, & are to be rendered to the war office, for the purpose of having the calculations made concurrently by the proper persons within the U.S. several copies of these, as well as your other notes, should be made at leisure times & and put into the care of the most trustworthy of your attendants, to guard by multiplying them, against the accidental losses to which they will be exposed. a further guard would be that one of these copies be written on the paper of the birch, as less liable to injury from damp than common paper.

The commerce which may be carried on with the people inhabiting the line you will pursue, renders a knolege of these people important. You will therefore endeavor to make yourself acquainted, as far as a diligent pursuit of your journey shall admit,

> with the names of the nations & their numbers;
> the extent & limits of their possessions;
> their relations with other tribes or nations;
> their language, traditions, monuments;
> their ordinary occupations in agriculture, fishing,
>   hunting, war, arts, & the implements for these;
> their food, clothing, & domestic accomodations;
> the diseases prevalent among them, & the remedies
>   they use;

moral & physical circumstances which distinguish
    them from the tribes we know;
peculiarities in their laws, customs & dispositions;
and articles of commerce they may need or furnish,
    & to what extent.

And considering the interest which every nation has
in extending & strengthening the authority of reason & jus-
tice among the people around them, it will be useful to
acquire what knolege you can of the state of morality, religion
& information among them, as it may better enable those
who endeavor to civilize & instruct them, to adapt their
measures to the existing notions & practices of those on whom
they are to operate.

Other objects worthy of notice will be

the soil & face of the country, it's growth & veg-
    etable productions; especially those not of the
    U.S.;
the animals of the country generally, & especially
    those not known in the U.S.;
the remains and accounts of any which may be
    deemed rare or extinct;
the mineral productions of every kind; but more
    particularly metals, limestone, pit coal & salt-
    petre; salines & mineral waters, noting the tem-
    perature of the last, & such circumstances as
    may indicate their character.
Volcanic appearances.
climate as characterized by the thermometer, by
    the proportion of rainy, cloudy & clear days, by
    lightning, hail, snow, ice, by the access & recess
    of frost, by the winds prevailing at different
    seasons, the dates of which particular plants put

forth or lose their flowers, or leaf, times of appearance of particular birds, reptiles or insects.

Altho' your route will be along the channel of the Missouri, yet you will endeavor to inform yourself, by inquiry, of the character & extent of the country watered by it's branches, & especially on it's southern side. the North river or Rio Bravo which runs into the gulph of Mexico, and the North river, or Rio Colorado, which runs into the gulph of California, are understood to be the principal streams heading opposite to the waters of the Missouri, and running Southwardly. whether the dividing grounds between the Missouri & them are mountains or flatlands, what are their distance from the Missouri, the character of the intermediate country, & the people inhabiting it, are worthy of particular enquiry. The Northern waters of the Missouri are less to be enquired after, because they have been ascertained to a considerable degree, and are still in a course of ascertainment by English traders & travellers; but if you can learn anything certain of the most Northern source of the Missisipi, & of it's position relative to the lake of the woods, it will be interesting to us. some account too of the path of the Canadian traders from the Missisipi, at the mouth of the Ouisconsin river, to where it strikes the Missouri and of the soil & rivers in it's course, is desirable.

In all your intercourse with the natives treat them in the most friendly & conciliatory manner which their own conduct will admit; allay all jealousies as to the object of your journey, satisfy them of it's innocence, make them acquainted with the position, extent, character, peaceable & commercial dispositions of the U.S. of our wish to be neighborly, friendly & useful to them, & of our dispositions to a commercial intercourse with them; confer with them on the

points most convenient as mutual emporiums, & the articles
of most desireable interchange for them & us. if a few of
their influential chiefs, within practicable distance, wish to
visit us, arrange such a visit with them, and furnish them
with authority to call on our officers, on their entering the
U.S. to have them conveyed to this place at public expence.
if any of them should wish to have some of their young
people brought up with us, & taught such arts as may be
useful to them, we will receive, instruct & take care of them.
such a mission, whether of influential chiefs, or of young
people, would give some security to your own party. carry
with you some matter of the kinepox, inform those of them
with whom you may be of it's efficacy as a preservative from
the small-pox; and instruct & incourage them in the use of
it. this may be especially done wherever you winter.

As it is impossible for us to foresee in what manner you
will be recieved by those people, whether with hospitality
or hostility, so it is impossible to prescribe the exact degree
of perserverance with which you are to pursue your journey.
we value too much the lives of citizens to offer them to
probable destruction. your numbers will be sufficient to se-
cure you again the unauthorised opposition of individuals, or
of small parties: but if a superior force, authorised or not
authorised, by a nation, should be arrayed against your further passage, & inflexibly determined to arrest it, you must
decline it's further pursuit, and return. in the loss of your-
selves, we should lose also the information you will have
acquired. by returning safely with that, you may enable us
to renew the essay with better calculated means. to your own
discretion therefore must be left the degree of danger you
may risk, & the point at which you should decline, only saying
we wish you to err on the side of your safety, & bring back
your party safe, even if it be with less information.

As far up the Missouri as the white settlements extend, an intercourse will probably be found to exist between them and the Spanish posts at St. Louis, opposite Cahokia, or Ste. Genevieve opposite Kaskaskia. from still farther up the river, the traders may furnish a conveyance for letters. beyond that you may perhaps be able to engage Indians to bring letters for the government to Cahokia or Kaskaskia, on promising that there they shall recieve such special compensation as you shall have stipulated with them. avail yourself of these means to communicate to us, at seasonable intervals, a copy of your journal, notes & observations of every kind, putting into cypher whatever might do injury if betrayed.

Should you reach the Pacific ocean inform yourself of the circumstances which may decide whether the furs of those parts may not be collected as advantageously at the head of the Missouri (convenient as is supposed to the waters of the Colorado & Oregon or Columbia) as at Nootka sound or any other point of that coast; & that trade be consequently conducted through the Missouri & U.S. more beneficially than by the circumnavigation now practiced.

On your arrival on that coast endeavor to learn if there be any port within your reach frequented by the sea-vessels of any nation, and to send two of your trusty people back by sea, in such way as shall appear practicable, with a copy of your notes. and should you be of opinion that the return of your party by the way they went will be eminently dangerous, then ship the whole, & return by sea by way of Cape Horn or the Cape of Good Hope, as you shall be able. as you will be without money, clothes or provisions, you must endeavor to use the credit of the U.S. to obtain them; for which purpose open letters of credit shall be furnished you authorizing you to draw on the Executive of the U.S. or any of its officers in any part of the world, on which drafts can be disposed of, and to apply with our recommendations to the Consuls, merchants, or citizens of any nation with whom we have intercourse, assuring them in our name that any aids they may furnish you, shall be honorably repaid, and on demand. Our consuls Thomas Hewes at Batavia in Java, William Buchanan on the isles of France and Bourbon, & John Elmslie at the Cape of Good Hope will be able to supply your necessities by draughts on us.

Should you find it safe to return by the way you go, after sending two of your party round by sea, or with your whole party, if no conveyance by sea can be found, do so; making such observations on your return as may serve to supply, correct or confirm those made on your outward journey.

In re-entering the U.S. and reaching a place of safety, discharge any of your attendants who may desire & deserve it, procuring for them immediate paiment of all arrears of pay & cloathing which may have incurred since their departure; & assure them that they shall be recommended to the liberality of the legislature for the grant of a soldier's portion of land each, as proposed in my message to Congress & repair yourself with your papers to the seat of government.

To provide, on the accident of your death, against anarchy, dispersion & the consequent danger to your party, and total failure of the enterprise, you are hereby authorised, by any instrument signed & written in your hand, to name the person among them who shall succeed to the command on your decease, & by like instruments to change the nomination from time to time, as further experience of the characters accompanying you shall point out superior fitness; and all the powers & authorities given to yourself are, in the

event of your death, transferred to & vested in the successor
so named, with further power to him, & his successors in
like manner to name each his successor, who, on the death
of his predecessor, shall be invested with all the powers &
authorities given to yourself.

Given under my hand at the city of Washington, this
20th day of June 1803.

TH. JEFFERSON
Pr. U.S. of America

Bibliography

ADAMS, HENRY. *History of the United States During the Administration of Thomas Jefferson.* 2 vols. New York: Albert and Charles Boni, 1930.

ALLEN, PAUL, editor. *History of the Expedition Under the Command of Captains Lewis and Clark . . . Performed During the Years 1804–5–6.* 2 vols. Philadelphia: Bradford and Inskeep, 1814. Reprinted by University Microfilms, Inc., Ann Arbor, Mich., 1966.

ANDERSON, JOHN J. *Did the Louisiana Purchase Extend to the Pacific Ocean?* New York: Clark & Maynard, 1881.

BAKELESS, JOHN. *Lewis and Clark: Partners in Discovery.* New York: William Morrow and Co., 1947.

BARBÉ-MARBOIS, FRANÇOIS, MARQUIS DE. *The History of Louisiana, Particularly the Cession of That Colony to the United States of America.* Translated from the French by "an American citizen." Philadelphia: Carey and Lea, 1830.

BIDDLE, NICHOLAS, *see* ALLEN, PAUL.

BROADHEAD, COL. JAMES O. "The Louisiana Purchase: Extent of Territory Acquired by the Said Purchase." Missouri Historical Society Collections, vol. 1, no. 13. St. Louis, 1897.

BROWN, EVERETT SOMERVILLE. *The Constitutional History of the Louisiana Purchase*. Berkeley: University of California Press, 1920.

BURROUGHS, RAYMOND D. *The Natural History of the Lewis and Clark Expedition*. Ann Arbor: University of Michigan Press, 1961.

CLARK, CHARLES G. "The Roster of the Lewis and Clark Expedition." *Oregon Historical Quarterly*, vol. 45, December, 1944.

CLARK, WILLIAM, *see* BIDDLE, ALLEN, COUES, THWAITES, DE VOTO, JACKSON, OSGOOD.

COUES, ELLIOTT, editor. *History of the Expedition Under the Command of Lewis and Clark*. 4 vols. New York: Francis P. Harper, 183.

CRISWELL, ELIJAH HARRY. "Lewis and Clark: Linguistic Pioneers." *The University of Missouri Studies*, vol. 15, no. 2, April 1940.

DARLING, ARTHUR BURR. *Our Rising Empire. 1763–1803*. New Haven: Yale University Press, 1940.

DE VOTO, BERNARD. *The Course of Empire*. Boston: Houghton Mifflin Company, 1952.

DE VOTO, BERNARD, editor. *The Journals of Lewis and Clark*. Boston: Houghton Mifflin Company, 1953.

DEACON, RICHARD. *Madoc and the Discovery of America: Some New Light on an Old Controversy*. New York: George Braziller, 1966.

DILLON, RICHARD. *Meriwether Lewis: A Biography*. New York: Coward-McCann, Inc., 1965.

FLOYD, CHARLES, *see* THWAITES, REUBEN GOLD.

FORD, PAUL LEICESTER, *see* JEFFERSON, THOMAS.

GANOE, WILLIAM ADDLEMAN. *The History of the United States Army*. New York and London: D. Appleton-Century Company, 1943.

GASS, PATRICK. *Gass' Journal of the Lewis and Clark Expedition*. Chicago: A. C. McClurg & Co., 1904.

GASS, PATRICK, *see also* COUES, ELLIOTT.

GAYARRE, CHARLES. *History of Louisiana: The American Domination*. 4 vols. New York: William J. Widdleton, 1866.

GEER, CURTIS MANNING. *The Louisiana Purchase and the Westward Movement*. Philadelphia: G. Barrie & Sons, 1904.

HAWGOOD, JOHN A. *America's Western Frontiers: The Exploration and Settlement of the Trans-Mississippi West*. New York: Alfred A. Knopf, 1967.

HODGE, F. W. *Handbook of American Indians North of Mexico*. 2 vols. Washington: Bureau of American Ethnology, 1907.

HOSMER, CHARLES K., editor. *History of the Expedition of Captains Lewis and Clark*. 2 vols. Chicago: A. C. McClurg & Co., 1924.

HOUCH, LOUIS. *The Boundaries of the Louisiana Purchase*. St. Louis: P. Roeder, 1901.

JACKSON, DONALD, editor. *Letters of the Lewis and Clark Expedition, with Related Documents, 1783–1854*. Urbana, Ill.: University of Illinois Press, 1962.

JEFFERSON, THOMAS. *The Writings of Thomas Jefferson*. Collected and edited by Paul Leicester Ford. 10 vols. New York: G. P. Putnam's Sons, 1897.

LANGFORD, NATHANIEL PITT. "The Louisiana Purchase and Preceding Spanish Intrigues for Dismemberment of the Union." Minnesota Historical Society Collections, vol. 9, St. Paul, 1901.

LAUT, AGNES C. *Pathfinders of the West*. New York: The Macmillan Company, 1904.

LEE, ROBERT EDSON. *From West to East: Studies in the Literature of the American West*. Urbana, Ill.: University of Illinois Press, 1966.

LEWIS, MERIWETHER, *see* BIDDLE, ALLEN, COUES, THWAITES, DE VOTO, QUAIFE, JACKSON, DILLON, WILSON.

LIGHTON, WILLIAM R. *Lewis and Clark*. Boston: Houghton, Mifflin Company, 1901.

NASATIR, A. P., editor. *Before Lewis and Clark: Documents Illustrating the History of the Missouri, 1785–1804*. 2 vols. St. Louis: St. Louis Historical Documents Foundation, 1952.

ORDWAY, JOHN, *see* QUAIFE, MILO M.

OSGOOD, ERNEST STAPLES, editor. *The Field Notes of Captain William Clark, 1803–1805*. New Haven: Yale University Press, 1964.

PHELPS, DAWSON A. "The Tragic Death of Meriwether Lewis." *The William and Mary Quarterly*, 3rd series, vol. XIII, no. 3, July, 1956.

QUAIFE, MILO M., editor. *The Journals of Captain Meriwether Lewis and Sergeant John Ordway, Kept on the Expedition of Western Exploration, 1803–1806.* Madison: State Historical Society of Wisconsin, 1916.

ROBERTSON, REV. CHARLES FRANKLIN. "The Attempts to Separate the West from the American Union." Missouri Historical Society Collections, vol. I, no. 10. St. Louis, 1885.

SALISBURY, ALBERT and JANE. *Two Captains West: An Historical Tour of the Lewis and Clark Trail.* Seattle: Superior Publishing Company, 1950.

SCHACHNER, NATHAN. *Thomas Jefferson, a Biography.* New York: Thomas Yoseloff, 1946.

SCHULTZ, JAMES WILLARD. *Bird Woman (Sacajawea), The Guide of Lewis and Clark.* Boston: Houghton Mifflin Company, 1918.

SKINNER, CONSTANCE L. *Adventurers of Oregon: A Chronicle of the Fur Trade.* New Haven: Yale University Press, 1921.

STEWART, GEORGE R. *Names on the Land.* New York: Random House, 1945.

STOUTONBURGH, JOHN, JR. *Dictionary of the American Indian.* New York: Philosophical Library, 1960.

THWAITES, REUBEN GOLD, editor. *Original Journals of the Lewis and Clark Expedition, 1804–1806.* 8 vols. New York: Dodd, Mead and Company, 1904–5.

TOMKINS, CALVIN. "The Lewis and Clark Case." *The New Yorker*, October 29, 1966.

WHEELER, OLIN D. *The Trail of Lewis and Clark.* 2 vols. New York: G. P. Putnam's Sons, 1904.

WHITEHOUSE, JOSEPH, *see* THWAITES, REUBEN GOLD.

WILSON, CHARLES MORROW. *Meriwether Lewis of Lewis and Clark.* New York: Thomas Y. Crowell Company, 1934.

Index